How dangerous men think

Brent Sanders

How dangerous men think

(and how to stay safe for life)

Brent Sanders

First published by Random House Australia & Random House New Zealand
in 2001

Random House Australia Pty Ltd
20 Alfred Street, Milsons Point, NSW 2061
http://www.randomhouse.com.au

Random House New Zealand
18 Poland Road, Glenfield, Auckland
http://www.randomhouse.co.nz

Sydney   New York   Toronto
London   Auckland   Johannesburg

National Library of Australia
Cataloguing-in-Publication Entry

Sanders, Brent.
How dangerous men think.

Bibliography
ISBN 0 091 84209 3

1. Self-defence for women. 2. Criminal psychology. I. Title.

613.66

Cover design by Gayna Murphy
Illustrations by Wayne Hutchins
Designed and typeset in New Century Schoolbook 11/12
by Midland Typesetters, Maryborough, Victoria
Printed and bound by Griffin Press, Netley, South Australia

10 9 8 7 6 5 4 3

The National Office of Rape Crisis New Zealand is pleased to
have the opportunity to endorse the book *How Dangerous Men
Think*. This book provides interesting insights into the way that
sexual offenders think, the way that they choose their intended
victims, and the most appropriate ways for women to use these
insights to defend themselves in potentially dangerous situations.
This book is well worth reading from cover to cover.

CONTENTS

Dedicated to the two most important people in my life, my wife Wendy and our daughter Molly. They are the inspiration and the motivation behind all that I do. May they stay safe for life.

INTRODUCTION

After 15 years of studying the ways sex offenders think, and showing women how to use that knowledge to stay safe, I know that the best self-protection device you will ever own is your mind. Whether it be sexual harassment, date rape, armed attack or gang confrontation, your best chance of walking away unharmed comes not from using Mace or employing a karate kick, but from knowing how your would-be assailant is thinking and using that against him. And that's why there are only a few pages in here devoted to the physical moves that usually make up the whole of self-defence books for women. I hope that when you've finished this book you, like the 60,000-plus women and girls to whom I have taught self-protection, agree that the real power lies in knowing how dangerous men think, and using that knowledge to protect yourself for life.

Rape is a male issue — it is *never* the fault of the woman or girl who is attacked. However, rape continues to happen, so women and girls need to know how to keep themselves safe. As a society we must ensure that sex offenders feel the full force of the law, and at the same time continue to study these offenders and pass this information on to those most likely to need it. We must understand how these dangerous men think in order to protect against them.

1

CONVERTING FEAR INTO POWER

Effective self-protection is developing the ability to control the way you think under pressure. The greatest weapon used against women in a conflict situation is their own fear. If you look at how offenders select their victims in any male to female confrontation, from verbal harassment through to sexual assault, you will see that the selection is based on the man's belief that the woman will react submissively because she is afraid. The offender feeds off this fearful, submissive reaction to achieve a feeling of power and control. That may not seem like news — every woman has encountered men who don't make any attempt to disguise this — and because of this it is easy to dismiss it as obvious and therefore of little use. But the crucial part is that the attacker *believes* his chosen victim will demonstrate her fear as submission. Knowing that is the first step in deciding not to become his victim. To take that step you need to understand your own fear. By understanding its causes, and developing the ability to control it, you can convert your own fear into an extremely powerful weapon which will protect you in any confrontation.

Understanding fear

The first step in controlling fear is to understand what *really* causes it. So often we hear people saying 'I'm terrified of being alone at night' or 'If I was being followed I'd just freeze,' or even worse 'If some guy grabbed me I'd be so terrified I wouldn't be able to do anything'. Most people would say that it's the *situation* that causes this fear. I disagree. We do not fear situations. What causes the fear is our *belief* that we do not have the ability to control them. This may not seem like much of a distinction, but bear with me and consider some common situations that evoke feelings of fear.

Imagine sitting in a seminar with 150 other women. After about half an hour the presenter informs the group he is going to select ten of you to do a 'retention test'. The test involves taking the ten outside, then bringing them back in one at a time to stand in front of the group and talk for two minutes on how much they remember about the introduction to the seminar. The presenter then walks around the group with a pen and paper selecting the ten unfortunates who will be taken outside. Imagine how you are feeling. What are the voices inside your head saying? 'Oh my God, don't let him pick me. I can't even remember his name, let alone anything else.' Or maybe 'Don't look at him! Look at the floor. Look away, look away.' And probably, 'It'll be me — I always get picked for these bloody things'. You have not only convinced yourself that you have been chosen, but also that you are going to fail miserably. The presenter then returns to the front of the room, takes one last look down at his list and says 'Before we go any further, there is just one last thing I need to tell you: the test is just a joke. I'm not going to get anyone to go outside and come back in to speak in front of the room; I'm having you on. Put your hand up if you have just experienced fear. Good. That's what we are going to talk about for the next half hour'.

I actually do this in all my seminars and the reaction is always the same. You can feel the tension in the room as you walk around to 'select' the ten people to take part in the 'test' and then the sheer relief when they realise it is only a joke. What the hell has this got to do with self-protection? Everything. Whether in a dark alleyway or in a seminar room, it's not the situation that causes the fear, but the attitude or belief that you bring to it.

Each person in the seminar room is gauging their ability to deal with the situation. Public speaking is recognised as people's greatest fear; in fact out of the top ten fears public speaking is number one, and death is number seven! Many people have convinced themselves they would rather die than talk in public. However, as with all our fears, it is not the act of public speaking that causes the fear but rather the *belief* that you will fail at it. Equally, with self-protection, the actual confrontation does not cause fear but rather the belief that you do not have the ability to take control and get out of danger.

Look back at any situation that you once feared, or felt nervous about, but that you no longer fear, and ask yourself this question: 'Has the *situation* changed?' I guarantee that it hasn't. What has changed is your belief in your ability to control the situation. I call this process bringing situations inside your 'comfort zone'. Inside your comfort zone is what you have achieved or believe you can achieve. Conversely, outside your comfort zone is what you have not yet achieved or believe you cannot achieve. The all-important first step in self-protection is bringing the concept inside your comfort zone, by believing that you have the ability to protect yourself in any type of confrontation and learning how to apply that belief in real situations.

Let's look at how this works in a potential confrontation. Imagine a woman walking alone down a dimly lit street late at night and discovering that she is being followed. Let us presume she is terrified of confrontation, and believes she does not have the ability to protect herself. Can you imagine her mental and physical reaction to this situation? She will initially ask herself the most commonly asked question in a confrontation: 'What do I have to do to get out of this?' If she is unable to answer this question she will mentally freeze; this is when the fear really starts to kick in. This frozen state of mind will invariably lead to the belief that the only option is to submit. What chance does she now have of taking control and getting to safety? Remember, it is not the situation which causes the fear. The offender is not causing the fear; he is merely anticipating it. The woman's fear and subsequent submission is directly related to the way she is *thinking* in the situation. If you believe you have no chance and no options then that is exactly what you have — no chance and no options. Put a different woman, one who knows how to protect herself and believes firmly in her ability to take control, into the same situation and the outcome may be totally different. This is *not* a criticism of women who've been attacked and who have not been able to take control of this type of confrontation effectively. But we can learn from those who *have* taken control of situations like this and got to safety. Without doubt, every girl and woman who has effectively taken control of a conflict situation to whom I have spoken over the past fifteen years of policing and lecturing has had one thing in common — they believed they could get out of the situation.

If the first step in controlling fear is recognising it is caused by what we believe rather than the situation itself, then the next step must be to look at what influences the way we think, and creates our belief systems.

Understanding our belief systems

What we *believe* is a direct result of what we frequently say to ourselves, together with what others frequently say to us. Bruce Lee, the martial arts master, often told his students 'Your mind is like a glass. The water in the glass is what you think you know. When you are born your glass is empty. As we get older we add water to the glass. If the glass becomes full there is no room for any more water. So if your mind becomes full of what you think you know, there is no room for any more knowledge'. He would suggest to his students that if their glass was full they should go away, pour out some of their water, then return and he would share some of his. I think this is a very good way of looking at knowledge.

Always remember that your mind leads your body. Often in the early stages of my seminars I have people say to me. 'But I couldn't get out of a conflict situation; I'd just freeze'. What they begin to realise is that with that belief system they are 100 per cent right. They would just freeze — because that is exactly what they have conditioned themselves to do. But it doesn't have to be that way.

Looking back at situations we have taken control over in the past, we can learn to apply the same skills to situations in the future. Remember, whether it's driving a car, riding a bike, operating a computer, public speaking or self-protection, the keys to success remain the same.

Take your mind back to when you first learnt to ride a bike. Imagine you have been tearing around on your tricycle and one morning you decide to have a crack at the two-wheeler that belongs to your big sister. Picture yourself standing in front of the bike as it rests along the garage door, trying to conjure up enough courage to have a go. Listen to the little voice on your shoulder: the voice of doubt, the voice of fear. Can you hear what it's saying? 'Don't get on the bike don't even try. Look at your legs; you'll never reach the pedals, Stumpy. Don't do it; you're too little; you'll fall off.'

But you want to have a go anyway. You take the bike by the handlebars and familiarise yourself with the equipment. All the time the little voice on your shoulder repeatedly tells you that you can't do it. Now for the moment of truth. You place the bike against the side of the house, take a deep breath and climb aboard. You sit rigidly in the saddle, legs outstretched, toes barely touching the pedals, one hand on the handlebar, the other gripping a handy windowsill. You are all set. You let go of the house, wobble uncontrollably, but somehow remain upright, and then rapidly grab once again for the relative safety of the windowsill. Maybe the voice on the shoulder was right; maybe you can't ride the bike. But what about all the other kids in the street? They seem to be able to master it; so why not you?

At this moment imagine Mum comes to lend a hand. She asks if you would like to be able to ride the bike. You say that you would but that you're experiencing some difficulty in the balancing department and therefore you can't do it. So Mum suggests that you hop off the bike, move it to the middle of the driveway and she will hold onto the back for you as you ride so you won't fall off. Brilliant! So you climb up onto the bike, both hands on the handlebars, quickly check to make sure she really is holding on and you're all set. Mum starts pushing. You start wobbling forward, slowly at first, but as Mum picks up the speed, as if by magic, the bike steadies and you're off down the driveway. At the end of the drive you guide the bike into a U-turn and back toward the garage you go. After a couple of trips up and down the drive the little voice on the shoulder that has been telling you that you can't do it gets quieter and quieter and is replaced by a voice on the other shoulder saying; 'This is great: I can ride the bike. As long as Mum holds on I can ride the bike'.

Of course you could ride the bike all the way across town if you believed Mum was holding on, but what you don't know is that Mum has already let go. She didn't tell you; she just kept running along behind the bike. She knew that as long as you *believed* she was holding on the fact that she had let go was not important. Now remember what happened when that pesky little voice on the shoulder came back and said, 'Hang on, I think Mum has let go. You had better turn around and check'. As you rode majestically down the driveway for the tenth time you assured yourself that all was well because Mum was, of course, holding on. 'But I'll have a quick look just in case.' So as your little legs continued to pedal for all they were worth you casually looked back over your shoulder to check. Horror of horrors — Mum had let go! Suddenly the bike develops a mind of its own, your legs turn to jelly and you let go of the handlebars.

So how did you end up in tears among the roses? The bike did not change, nor did the laws of gravity, and Mum had actually let go about five minutes earlier. What changed, of course, was your belief. The moment you said, 'I can't do this', your mind accepted the information and the rest is history.

Even as children we proved to ourselves that the power of the mind is far greater than any situation we are confronted with. We were also being taught that the mind is a double-edged sword and will work just as powerfully for us as against us. The decision is yours.

People like Kirsty Marshall, the Australian aerial skiing champion and winner of more than 30 world championship medals, know this well. Kirsty was once asked in an interview to identify the key to her success. She replied 'The key to my success was the moment I realised that my body can only achieve what my mind can perceive. You must first *believe* it before you can achieve it.'

The keys to succeeding in a self-protection situation are really no different to those in any other situation.

So far we have looked at what actually causes fear. We have also looked at what influences the way we think and in turn creates our belief systems. Now let's discuss one of the most important ingredients of all when it comes to effective self-protection — *motivation*.

Understanding motivation

It has been said that if success is the destination, then motivation is the fuel needed to get you there. If you look at your own achievements in life you'll find it is your *motivation* that has driven you to succeed. In the same way, in a conflict situation victory always belongs to those most motivated to win.

While conducting one of my seminars I once witnessed one of the greatest examples of the power of motivation I have ever seen. I was presenting my message in a half-day seminar to 30 female employees of a large city corporation. During the presentation I spoke about the importance of positive thinking, self-motivation and fear management, along with the psychology of offenders and strategies for dealing with confrontation ranging from verbal harassment through to sexual assault. We concluded the seminar with a short session on physical strikes. I was returning the following week to discuss weapons, gangs and a range of other situations. At the conclusion of this first session I thanked the participants for attending and said I looked forward to seeing them all the following week. As I packed my notes away I was approached by one of the women attending the course. The conversation we had over the following five to ten minutes is one I've never forgotten.

The woman, let's call her Mary, told me that she had come into the room three hours earlier believing that she could never defend herself. I appreciated her honesty and assumed that she was about to tell me everything had changed and she could now effectively deal with any of the situations we had covered during the course. How wrong I was. Mary went on to tell me that not only was her attitude unchanged but that the course was, in fact, an absolute waste of time. She thought none of this 'positive thinking crap' worked in the real world and no way was she coming back next week to listen to more of this garbage. As you can appreciate, I was a little taken aback, so in an attempt to buy some time, I asked Mary if she could, perhaps, expand on her less than glowing evaluation of my presentation. Mary told me she was 32 years old and, thankfully, had never been attacked but if she was there was nothing she could do about it anyway and this course had not changed that fact!

At this stage I was reminded of Bruce Lee's remarks about the mind being like a glass of water mentioned earlier. Mary's glass was so full of negativity there was no room for anything else. I decided to see if I could still change that. I asked Mary if she could actually give me an example of a confrontational situation that she would be unable to get out of. She said 'I'll give you a bloody example all right!', and pointed towards the door. I have no doubt this example had been on Mary's mind all morning. She said 'If I walked out that door now, got into the lift and went down to the basement to get my car, and some bloke was to jump out and grab me, I couldn't defend myself. I couldn't suddenly become all motivated, think positively and miraculously get out of the situation. I'd just freeze. I wouldn't be able to do anything and none of this stuff you're going on about would make any difference.' The problem was that Mary actually believed this, and with 32 years of negative conditioning to support her belief, I am not surprised. I told Mary I was sorry for wasting three hours of her time but if she could give me just a few more minutes I might be able to sort something out. She reluctantly agreed.

We sat down and I again asked her to discuss her feelings about the course. She talked for a few more minutes about how motivation does not work, how you can't change the way you think and that's that. After a couple of minutes, I asked her if she was married. She said she was. I asked her if she had any children. She told me she had a little girl who was eighteen months old. I asked her to tell me about her daughter. Suddenly Mary become 'Mum': her whole facial expression changed, her body language relaxed and she spoke lovingly about her little daughter. (As the father of a little girl I can understand this. Having a child has been described as growing another heart, an analogy most parents can relate to.) After chatting about her daughter for a couple of minutes and looking at the photographs that materialised from Mary's wallet, I asked her to imagine that her daughter was in the room with us. I told her to imagine that she was now leaving with her daughter, walking across the training room, through the hall and into the lift. Once in the lift I asked Mary to imagine lifting her daughter up so she could press the 'B' button which would take them down to the basement. I was about to put Mary back into the situation she had spent the last five to ten minutes telling me she couldn't get out of. The only difference was that this time she would be in the situation with her daughter.

I asked Mary to imagine the lift had reached the basement, the doors had opened and she was now walking through the basement with her daughter to collect her car. I told her to picture herself holding her little girl's hand and to imagine that just as they are about to reach the car she hears the screeching of tyres behind them. She turns around to see a man jumping out of the car in a black balaclava, black T-shirt, jeans and a pair of runners. The man is running toward her, but he doesn't want Mary — he wants her little girl. Before I tell you what I said next to Mary please bear in mind that, through her own admission, Mary had believed for 32 years that she was incapable of defending herself, or anyone else, in any type of physical confrontation.

I told Mary that if she did not protect her daughter the man would grab her and take her back to his car. I got Mary to imagine her little girl being taken away by this stranger. I told her to think about how frightened her daughter would be and to imagine her being thrown into the car, crying in the back seat as the car disappeared out of the car park. I told Mary this man would take her daughter away and do terrible things to her and that she might never see her again. I then asked, 'Mary, what are you going to do to this guy?' She said 'I'll kill him!' I asked, 'How would you do that, exactly?' Well, not only did she tell me, she leapt up off her chair and gave me a very graphic illustration of how she would do it.

She started screaming and punching viciously out at the imaginary kidnapper before he could grab her daughter. She threw him to the floor, grabbed a handful of hair and, still screaming, showed me how she would repeatedly smash the guy's face into the concrete floor again and again. She concluded this frighteningly lifelike defence of her daughter by getting back to her feet and repeatedly kicking the offender's face, head, stomach and groin. I thanked Mary and very quietly asked her if she would like to sit down. Even as she sat down her fists were still clenched.

When she had calmed down a little I asked her the obvious question: 'Mary, ten minutes ago you told me that if you went down to the basement and some guy grabbed you, you would be absolutely helpless, totally unable to defend yourself and nothing I could say would make any difference to that. Now you're fighting back like a Ninja! What happened?' Mary looked up from the ground after a few moments with a wide grin and said 'Brent, I could defend myself, couldn't I?' I said 'Yes, if you believe it.' Charged with this realisation, she got up off her seat and confidently strode toward the door shouting out 'Yes! Yes!' punching her fists triumphantly into the air as she made her way down to the basement. It was great to witness that transformation — and the power it brought with it.

Mary's story highlights many important aspects of self-protection. Did she just suddenly develop the ability to physically defend herself and her daughter? No; the ability was always there; she simply tapped into it by getting *motivated*. For most of her life Mary believed she was incapable of physically defending herself. Whenever she imagined being in a confrontational situation she had a picture of herself failing. All I did was change the mental picture. Rather than seeing herself being attacked I persuaded Mary to imagine her daughter was the one in danger. At that moment her motivation to succeed was greater than her fear of failing and, in a heartbeat, a lifetime of negative conditioning disappeared. Not only did Mary realise she had the ability to protect her little girl, but to protect herself too.

I honestly believe every person reading this book has the ability to protect herself in any type of confrontation. You are born with this ability, as you are with the instinctive urge to defend yourself against danger. In nature it is generally the female who fiercely protects her young and trains them to defend themselves and how to hunt.

I think Mary's story offers a great lesson. At times we all allow ourselves to fall into the trap of believing we can't do this or we can't do that and we pay the price. As Henry Ford put it, Whether a person thinks they can, or whether a person thinks they can't, they are always right.

Once we have the ability to control the way we *think* about a situation we have the ability to control it. The keys to successful self-protection are the same as the keys to success in every other aspect of life: having a goal, knowing how to achieve it, believing in your ability to succeed and the motivation to win.

The keys to succeed

1. The first key to success is having a *goal*. You must have a goal in mind in order to achieve anything.
2. Once the goal is established, you must know how to achieve it. This *knowledge* leads to the third key:
3. Having the *belief* in your own ability to achieve your goal.
4. When you have the knowledge to achieve your goal and you believe in your own ability to achieve it you create the fourth and final key to success — *motivation*. And with a goal, knowledge, belief and motivation nothing — and nobody — can stop you.

This sounds all very well, but how does it apply to you?

Imagine you are walking alone down a suburban street when out of the blue a car pulls up and suddenly a guy jumps out and grabs you — his intention is to abduct and rape you. Let's apply the four keys to success to this situation. Your *goal* is obviously to get away from the guy, and your *knowledge* tells you to yell at the top of your voice and physically repel him (the strategies for dealing with an unarmed stranger confrontation are covered in detail in Chapter Three). You *believe* you have the ability to do what is required and, most importantly, you are *motivated* to succeed. If your motivation to get away is greater than the offender's motivation to get you into the car, you will win. Never lose sight of the fact that the offender has selected you with the 100 per cent belief that you will be so scared of him you will just freeze and offer little or no resistance.

I have spoken to many women who have been in this type of confrontation and have effectively taken control by simply being more focused and more motivated than the offender.

Self-protection is primarily a mental process rather than a physical one. Physical acts of self defence are not difficult once the mind is focused to succeed.

Summary

The ability to convert fear into power is the first step in effective self-protection. By recognising that fear is not caused by the situation, but rather by how we think in that situation, we see it is essential to have a positive, focused mind-set in any confrontation. Once we are aware of this we start to understand the importance of believing in our ability. This leads us to the all-important ingredient of success — motivation. When we are motivated we can take control of any situation that confronts us; life is made up of ten per cent of what happens to you and 90 per cent of how you *think* about what happens to you.

Five steps to converting fear into power

The following steps are extremely effective in converting fear into power in both day-to-day and potentially confrontational situations. Try them the next time you feel nervous or apprehensive about your ability to take control.

1. Be aware of how you are feeling. Get in touch with what your body is telling you.
2. Ask yourself, 'Why do I feel like this?' Explore the reasons and identify exactly what it is that you are dreading.
3. Recognise the fear for what it is and know that you can change the way you feel. Your mind guides your body: *if you think it, you feel it.* If you think you have to be afraid your mind tells the rest of your body how to feel.

4. Change your mind-set; change the message. Tell yourself that you are not afraid, you are in control. Motivate yourself to reject the negative and accept the positive. Teach yourself to be positive. Tell yourself, 'I am in control', 'I am confident and will succeed'.

5. Feel the power. The moment you decide to believe that you are not afraid, you are confident and in control, you will have converted your feelings of fear into power. This process works because what you think determines what you feel and what you feel determines your attitude and your attitude determines the outcome of every situation you are confronted with.

2

SEXUAL HARASSMENT AND THE MALE MIND-SET

Once we understand how to control the way *we* think in a pressure situation the next step is to understand exactly what our opponent is thinking. The best way to see destructive men's thought processes in action is to look at a situation of sexual harassment — the most common form of attack against women. Once you understand this you can understand every form of male to female confrontation.

Sexual harassment

Sexual harassment is unlawful under the Federal Sex Discrimination Act of 1984, and under State and Territory laws throughout Australia. The Federal Sex Discrimination Act defines sexual harassment as: 'An unwelcome sexual advance; or an unwelcome request for sexual favours; or unwelcome conduct of a sexual nature if the behaviour takes place in circumstances in which a reasonable person would have anticipated that the person would have felt offended; or humiliated; or intimidated.' Basically that means that any behaviour toward you of a sexual nature that makes you feel uncomfortable is sexual harassment.

In New Zealand sexual harassment is covered by the Human Rights Act of 1993 and the Harassment Act of 1997. The situation is a little different from Australia in that it is unlawful when a request for sex is combined with a promise or a threat, or when behaviour of a sexual nature causes a detrimental effect on the victim. The Harassment Act prohibits conduct which causes the victim to fear for her safety.

Let's look at how sexual harassment works. The first thing to note is that not everybody is targeted for this type of confrontation. I have been around for over thirty years but have never been sexually harassed, yet I do not know of one woman over the age of 15 who has not experienced sexual harassment! The reason for this is so obvious it is often overlooked.

Girls and women are selected as targets because the harasser believes that they will react the 'right' way. I am rejected as a target because I probably would not react in this way.

The desired response is one that makes the harasser look and feel powerful. This is either total submission or, at the opposite end of the spectrum, an over-reaction such as crying, screaming or yelling. Either of these responses will give the guy the feeling of power and control he is seeking from the confrontation. And if he gets the response he is looking for the harassment will continue and may intensify.

Without doubt one of the most disturbing comments I hear during my seminars comes from young women who say 'What's the point of trying to do anything about a guy hassling you? It will only make it worse'. Sadly they have just identified *why* they are selected; this is exactly the mind-set the guys are hoping for.

If society conditions young women to think they have no option but to accept harassment then we allow them to believe that standing up for themselves and being assertive is not only undesirable but is actually beyond their capability. This simply plays into the hands of those who exploit the weakness of others to make themselves feel powerful.

One of the things that concerns me most about allowing blatant sexual harassment to go unchecked is this: if a woman believes she is unable to stand up for herself in a verbal confrontation, what chance does she have of getting out of a physical confrontation? I believe self-protection is just as important in situations of verbal sexual harassment as it is in sexual assault. The old adage 'just ignore them and they will go away' unfortunately doesn't work in this situation and may set a dangerous precedent for more threatening confrontations.

The key to effectively dealing with sexual harassment, as with any form of confrontation, it is your ability to 'get inside the head' of the person you're dealing with. You must understand *why* you have been selected and *what* he is expecting you to do. Only then are you in a position to select the best strategy to use against him.

Sexual harassment, like every form of male to female confrontation, is *never* an expression of genuine strength. Even if it involves physical strength, it is always an expression of weakness, as the attacker tries to gain the power he feels he lacks.

So before we look at a typical situation and how to deal with it let's sum up the harasser's selection process and the motivation behind every incident of sexual harassment.

Summary

- Women are selected for harassment because they are perceived as good targets.
- A 'good target' is a person who will respond in a way that makes the harasser look and feel powerful.
- If the harasser gets the response he is looking for, either submission or over-reaction, the situation will probably continue and usually get worse.
- Men who sexually harass women are attempting to compensate for a feeling of weakness and inadequacy.

Let's look now at a typical scenario for sexual harassment in a social environment.

Sexual harassment scenario

It is a Friday night. You are out at a bar in the city with two or three girlfriends enjoying a girls' night out. You all decide to visit the toilet located at the far end of the bar. Standing outside the women's toilet is a group of guys. In among the group is the guy we mentioned earlier. Let's call him the Dickhead. He spends a great part of his life seeking out those whom he perceives to be weaker than himself. He continually harasses those whom he believes will submit to him. He attempts to compensate for his numerous inadequacies by constructing a thin veneer of power and confidence. Every bar, every nightclub, every party, every workplace and every classroom has a Dickhead, and they all play the same game the same way.

You and your friends walk past the group and into the toilet. After a few minutes one of your girlfriends heads out past the group of guys and back to where you have been sitting. This provides an opportunity for the Dickhead which is too good to miss: a bar full of people, him with all his mates and a woman on her own who looks to him like she's just asking to be hassled. In his mind he puts a big sign above your head; 'I'm a woman pick on me.'

Our friend turns to his mates and says, 'Watch this boys, this will really crack you up.' He then walks up behind your girlfriend and suddenly is all over her like a rash. His hands grope her everywhere as he rubs himself up against her and announces to the bar, 'Hey darling, you like a bit of this, don't you. Hey, boys what do you reckon, give her one or what?' At this stage imagine your girlfriend responds by saying quietly, almost in a whisper, 'Don't. Just stop it; don't.' She then slinks off back to the other side of the bar amidst great hilarity from our mate and his friends.

If we freeze the scenario right there we can see this is a classic illustration of a typical sexual harassment confrontation:

- Guy selects girl because he perceives her to be a good target.
- Girl responds submissively, which reinforces in the guy's mind he has made a good choice.
- The situation continues and gets worse for the girl. She walks away feeling embarrassed and defeated.
- The guy goes back to his mates as the big hero. Once again he has compensated for a feeling of inadequacy by selecting a target who has submitted to him.
- Whether the scene is a bar, a classroom, a party or a workplace the 'game' is always the same.
- The cycle continues.

Now let's have some fun. Let's imagine you come out of the bathroom and are confronted in exactly the same way.

As you walk through the bar our friend approaches you from behind and verbally and physically confronts you. Obviously confident from his previous encounter, he lets fly with all the usual bar-room banter followed by the regulation grope and pelvic thrust.

You stop and slowly turn around to confront him. A hush of anticipation falls upon the bar. But before responding, you ask yourself the two most important questions you can ever ask yourself in a conflict:

1. 'Why have I been selected?'
2. 'What is he expecting me to do?'

Asking these questions not only gets you inside the head of the person who has confronted you, but is also a very effective way to identify and target the weakness of your opponent. Identifying your opponent's weakness is the key behind every form of effective self-protection, whether it is verbal or physical.

Having asked the questions, let's answer them. You have been selected for this confrontation simply because you are a woman and therefore seen as a good target. The guy who has selected you expects one of two reactions: you will either submit completely or 'over-react' by becoming visibly distressed. Both of these reactions provide the guy with a feeling of power and control.

Having identified the selection process behind the confrontation you now choose how to react.

Rather than reacting the way you are expected to by either shying away from the situation or, conversely, yelling, screaming and making a big scene, imagine, just for fun, you choose the following reaction.

Facing him and maintaining eye contact you quietly reach forward with your right hand, palm skyward, fingers slightly separated, almost claw-like, and with the speed and grace of an eagle you grab a handful of testicles! Your eyes never leave his as the colour slowly drains from his cheeks and a strange animal-like whimper emanates from the back of his throat. The group of friends who, not ten seconds earlier, were in full verbal support of their heroic comrade have fallen silent and ashen-faced. Your grip tightens.

There is no word to describe the pain this would cause. It is so excruciatingly painful that once you have experienced it just seeing it happen to somebody else makes you feel sick.

As the bar falls silent, you quietly lean forward and say, 'Next time I walk past you, if you touch me or make any comment, I'll rip these off and shove them fair up your arse!' You then confidently stroll back to your girlfriends.

Now, I know what's going through your mind. How can anybody suggest to an intelligent, rational-thinking person that this is the most effective way to deal with sexual harassment? Well, of course I am not suggesting that at all; we are just exploring possible reactions. Far be it for me to suggest the next time some bloke verbally and physically confronts you in a social environment you grab a fistful of his genitalia. But let's look at the all-important end result.

An hour later the girls need to visit the bathroom again. You all walk through the bar and back past the Dickhead and his mates. Which one of your group will not be hassled? The answer is fairly obvious. The reason you are no longer seen as a good target is because you stood up for yourself. You didn't submit or yell and scream. Rather, you confronted your harasser and targeted his weakness, in this instance a physical one. And the end result is that you are no longer perceived as a good target.

But we agree that this method is too drastic. So how

about learning a strategy that almost guarantees the same end result but requires absolutely no verbal or physical contact with the harasser? A strategy I have taught to over 60,000 girls and women? A strategy that *not one* girl or woman who has used it has come back and told me didn't work? A strategy that immediately puts you in control?

Before we move forward, let us briefly summarise:

Summary

- The first girl selected reacted exactly as the Dickhead anticipated, which made him look and feel powerful in front of his mates.
- He selected you, anticipating the same submissive response.
- Your response, however, was totally unexpected. And because you confronted him and took control of the situation, the likelihood of being selected as his victim again is minimal.
- Remember, no matter what form the confrontation takes, the way you respond will do one of two things. It will encourage the situation to continue or it will convince your harasser to stop.
- The two key questions to ask in any conflict situation are, '*Why* have I been selected?' and, '*What* does he expect me to do?'

Now let us examine a strategy for dealing with sexual harassment that encompasses all the keys of effective self-protection.

The 'dog on the couch' strategy

I have been teaching the 'dog on the couch' strategy so long I can't actually remember how it originated.

To fully appreciate how the strategy works I must first tell you a quick story about a dog — one of those dogs that is always trying to get up on the couch where he knows he's not allowed. Once we have done this we can compare the behaviour of the dog to that of the Dickhead.

Imagine you're sitting at home watching TV when your dog comes in. You give him a quick pat and go back to watching your program. The dog makes his way across the lounge room towards the couch. At this stage in the back of your mind you're thinking 'He'd better not get up on the couch. He knows he's not allowed on the couch.'

The dog is now standing alongside the couch. He knows what he is about to do is wrong, but he thinks that with you he'll get away with it. *Start to compare the dog to the Dickhead.* The dog has a sly look over his shoulder and sees you're watching the TV. He seems to be thinking 'Bugger it, I'll have a go!' He quickly jumps up onto the couch.

At this moment you have a choice. You could get up out of your chair, walk across to the couch and firmly instruct the dog to get down and go outside, which would almost certainly work. Or you could simply choose to ignore what the dog is doing and go back to watching the TV. Let's say you do exactly that. You ignore the dog and go back to watching the TV.

Back on the couch the dog will now make a decision

on what to do next. Does he know he is not supposed to be sitting on the couch? Yes. So he knows what he is doing is wrong? Yes. Did he think, however, that with you he could get away with it? Yes. Was he right? Yes. Does he now get off the couch? NO. The dog will now take full advantage of the situation, roll over and go to sleep. The situation has become worse and is continuing. *Compare the dog to the Dickhead.*

The following night you're sitting watching the TV and again the dog walks in but tonight you detect a subtle difference in his attitude. He is no longer apprehensive about getting up on the couch; in fact, tonight he thinks he owns the place! He strolls across the lounge room full of attitude and bad manners and bang, straight up onto the couch and off to sleep. *Compare the dog to the Dickhead.*

Tonight you think you had better do something about this situation. But, of course, as anybody who has a dog would know, you can tell the dog a thousand times not to get up on the couch and he won't. However, let him get away with it once and you can forget the thousand times you said 'No'.

You have a go anyway. You leap from the comfort of your chair and stride confidently across the lounge room to confront the dog, now apparently fast asleep on the couch. In loud guttural tones as described in every 'dog-training' manual you announce to the dog 'Nooooooooooo!' which is met with the slow, lazy lifting of one eyelid. You repeat the command, louder and longer.

Undaunted by your lack of success, you continue with

the verbal commands and all the classic finger-pointing action designed to direct the dog off the couch and outside: 'No, get down! Down! Get off the couch! Get out — outside; go out; down, down!' But, unfortunately, all this is coming a little too late. The dog believes he is quite entitled to do what he is doing and has no intention of moving. Finally you resort to giving him a clip across the ear and tell him one last time to get down. The dog reluctantly does so. Order is, at last, restored.

What the hell has all this got to do with sexual harassment? Well, if we apply the dog's behaviour to a typical sex harassment scenario there are some interesting comparisons.

Imagine being at a party or social function with a group of female friends, all of whom are familiar with the 'dog on the couch' strategy. At some point in the evening imagine you are standing chatting with your friends when you are suddenly targeted for a fairly generous serving of verbal harassment from an unknown male guest.

At this stage I believe you have a limited number of options available to you. If you would like the situation to continue, simply ignore it or over-react and you will play right into the hands of the harasser. However, if you would prefer to take total control of the situation and make the guy look like a complete imbecile, you may wish to try the 'dog on the couch' strategy.

Remember, you have been selected because you are a woman and he expects you to submit or totally over-react. Remember, never do what they expect you to do!

Now the fun starts. Put your drink down, turn around

and look at him. Do not say or do a thing. Hands on hips is good; not compulsory, but you can throw it in if you like. Resist the urge to say anything; at this stage silence is your greatest weapon. Observe what is happening around the room. Everybody has gone very quiet; they start to look like they're at a tennis match. They look at you, they look at the guy, then back to you, then back to the guy.

Now observe the bloke who has selected you. One very valuable lesson I learnt as a policeman was, when in a conflict situation, *never listen to what they're saying, but rather look at what they're thinking*. Get inside their head by reading their body language. Look at his body language and it will tell you this guy believes he has total control over the situation and you will respond exactly the way he expects you to. The other thing I would like you to observe is that most guys in this type of situation have one, maximum two 'good' lines they can use. *What they say is not important; what is important is how you respond.*

Once the guy has your full attention he will get set to deliver the first of his two 'lines' which, of course, are designed to get you verbally involved. He turns to his mates and says, 'Watch this, boys this will really wind her up'. And then comes the first line.

Whatever he says, *say and do nothing*; just keep staring at him, but give him nothing. If you look closely you will observe a subtle but interesting change in body language. Our friend is not too sure what's going on. The little voice in his head is saying, 'This isn't working. What's happening here. This isn't funny.' But he can't turn back now, he has too much to lose. He has one line left; this always gets a reaction; this is sure to impress his mates. He throws this line at you. Stand your ground; give him nothing to work with. *Say nothing; just keep staring at him.*

Now look at his body language. Our friend now realizes he has made a mistake in selecting you. You're not reacting the right way. But he has come too far and has nowhere to go. He is begging for you to respond. He looks nervously around the room; all eyes are on him, but he has run out of steam, he has nothing left to say.

At this point focus on the body language and try not to laugh; the fun has just begun. I now want you to focus on something just above his head. It's a big sign: DICK-HEAD — and the longer he stands there the brighter it gets! Now I want you to think about your dog and say to yourself 'This guy is just like my dog'. Why is he just like your dog? Well,

- When your dog gets up on the couch he knows what he is doing is wrong. Likewise when this guy stands in front of a room full of people and verbally abuses you he knows what he is doing is wrong.
- But the dog thinks he will get away with it with you, just like our friend at the party.
- If you sit watching the TV you are doing exactly what the dog wanted you to do so the situation will continue and get worse. If you respond to sexual harassment the way the harasser wants you to by either submitting or over-reacting, he too will continue and the situation will get worse.
- If you let the dog sit on the couch on Monday, Tuesday,

Wednesday, Thursday and then try to get him off on Friday you can't — he thinks he owns the couch. Try ignoring, submitting, or 'over-reacting' to sexual harassment once, twice, three times and then try to stop it. Just like the dog's behaviour it becomes more and more difficult to control.

▪ The key to controlling the dog's behaviour is identifying *what* the dog is doing, *why* he is doing it and sorting it out straight away before he thinks he is in control. *Compare the dog to the Dickhead.*

Stay with me now, we're almost there! Once you have made the indisputable comparison between the dog and the Dickhead I would ask you to take the all-important final step in the strategy. Simply imagine or visualise the guy in front of you standing there in a big dog suit. Just see him in a dog suit and now start to giggle, then let the giggle turn into a polite chuckle, the chuckle into a chortle and finally really let yourself go and have a bloody good laugh.

One of your girlfriends is chatting with another guest and has missed all of this but now hears you laughing and turns around. She is well aware of the 'dog on the couch' strategy so knows exactly what's going on and races over to join you. She too is laughing aloud, pointing to the guy and saying, 'It's him; look, it's the dog, I knew it was going to be him!' A third friend who is equally well versed in this unique strategy now joins you and joins in with the hilarity and points knowingly at our somewhat bemused friend.

How is the guy dealing with this? Not well, I can assure you. In the nine years I have taught this strategy the most common response at this point is the guy standing in front of a room full of very amused onlookers with an embarrassed and stupid look on his face offering feeble resistance such as, 'Don't. Stop it. That's really stupid, don't', usually followed up by a hasty retreat. The likelihood of further harassment from this individual has just plummeted. You are no longer perceived as a good target because 'good targets' don't make their harassers look and feel ridiculous as you have just done. Of course some guys may attempt to regain a level of control by throwing a few insults at you, such as 'What are you laughing at, you stupid . . . ' My advice would be to recognise this response for what it is — a desperate attempt to engage you in a verbal slanging match — so just stand your ground and keep laughing. Don't mistake his response as being one of strength. I can assure you it is motivated by weakness and a fear of being confronted.

Although not as physically painful as the aforementioned 'squirrel grip' the end result is no less effective.

At this point I am reminded of a recent seminar I conducted at a high school. I had just taught the 'dog on the couch' strategy to 100 very enthusiastic 17-year-old girls and was about to give them a 15 minute break. As I looked down at my watch, I was interrupted by yelling, screaming and taunting coming from a group of 50 or more 17-year-old boys outside. The verbal assault was obviously being directed at the girls in an attempt to intimidate or offend them. I told the girls they had no choice but to confront the group, as there was only one exit available. I reminded them that they had a choice about how they responded, but to bear in mind submission or over-reaction would only make the situation worse. I suggested they try the strategy I had just taught them; what did they have to lose? My advice was to go outside and, if confronted, put your hands on your hips, look the guy up and down, think about your dog and crack up! So out they went.

The first thing I heard was all the blokes, 'Blah, blah, self-defence crap, blah, blah, girls have got no idea, blah, blah'. The next thing I heard were shrieks of laughter and I then looked up to see more than 100 girls running back into the gym screaming, 'It works, it works, oh my God, it works!' Needless to say that was the last we heard of the boys for the remainder of the day.

Summary

The key to the 'dog on the couch' strategy is that it follows the basic philosophy behind effective self-protection: Don't focus on your opponent's strength and submit to it, but rather, identify his weakness and target that. There is one thing the next guy that harasses you is totally unprepared for, one thing he is paranoid about, one thing he has absolutely no defence for: being laughed at. If you don't believe it, simply try it and join the thousands of other women who have discovered the key to dealing with the most common form of male to female conflict: sexual harassment.

Sexual harassment is not only present in social settings but also in the workplace, school, university, and other learning/teaching institutions. In fact the law regarding sexual harassment was designed for these very environments and if it occurs you are entitled, by law, to make a formal complaint either via internal channels or directly to the Anti-Discrimination Board in your state or the Human Rights Commission in New Zealand.

If you are targeted for any form of sexual harassment at work or within any educational institution I would suggest you initially inform the person harassing you that their behaviour is unwelcome and that you want it to stop. If you are not comfortable doing this or your requests have fallen on deaf ears, I suggest you take the next step which is to speak with the person within the organisation who is designated to deal with complaints of this nature, such as the Equal Opportunities Officer, Human Resources Officer or Sexual Harassment Complaints Officer. Positions such as these are mandatory in large corporations, public service and educational institutions in Australia and are commonly found in New Zealand.

If you do not wish to discuss the matter with somebody within your organisation, or your organisation does not have such a person, you can always contact an external group such as your union, State Anti-Discrimination Board or the Human Rights and Equal Opportunity Commission (the Human Rights Commission in New Zealand). These organisations generally provide a free advisory service for such matters.

Understanding and dealing effectively with sexual harassment is not only extremely empowering but also serves as a great foundation for dealing with all forms of male to female conflict. The 'dog on the couch' strategy, although it may strike you as somewhat bizarre, is very effective simply because it identifies and targets your opponent's weakness and in turn protects you from further confrontation. It need not be carried out exactly to the letter, but the philosophy behind it should be understood. As you read through the following chapters many of the basic elements of sexual harassment are expanded upon as we examine more volatile forms of conflict.

Look back over your own life and recall experiences where you have been targeted for the type of harassment we have discussed in this chapter. Look at how you have responded to these situations and identify whether the situation has *continued* or been *controlled*. Now look at the pattern. I guarantee the situations you have 'ignored' or submitted to have continued and become worse. Conversely, those you have stood up to and confronted are invariably those you have taken control of.

Just remember the next time you are selected for any form of sexual harassment, the guy believes you are a good target. Whether you are will be determined by the way you respond. You *can* take control.

3

THE PSYCHOLOGY OF THE STRANGER RAPIST

Having looked at verbal confrontation in a typical harassment scenario we will now explore physical confrontation in sexual assault. This chapter will take you inside the mind of a typical stranger rapist or serial rapist to reveal his motivation, selection process, methods, strengths and weaknesses and we will look at the findings of numerous independent studies into rape psychology round the world. With these insights we will identify the most effective strategies to employ against this type of offender.

There is no strategy that works every time in any given situation. The best strategy, therefore, is the one most *likely to work* in the particular situation you are in. In this chapter we will examine the options you have so that you can identify the best course of action when you need to defend yourself.

Profile of a typical stranger rapist

*Practitioners and social scientists are gradually learning much of the rapist's art and cunning. The more their victims and potential victims acquire of this knowledge the more **power** they will possess against them.*

Dr William Glaser
Department of Psychiatry, University of Melbourne
'Without Consent' conference, Melbourne, 1992

Profiling of sexual offenders is common police practice throughout the world and is recognised as one of the most effective methods of identifying and apprehending serial offenders. Movies like *Silence of the Lambs* have shown in a fairly realistic way how organisations such as the FBI go about this.

In 1991 I began to profile known serial sex offenders from a slightly different perspective. My profiling was designed to look into the case studies of these offenders to identify their selection processes in order to work out *what strategies consistently worked against them*. The more cases I studied the more clearly I could identify the pattern I was seeking. This pattern convinced me beyond any doubt that knowledge of how the offender thinks, plus the appropriate strategy for the situation, are the essential ingredients in dealing effectively with a rape confrontation.

I have often been asked if there is one effective strategy to deal with all types of sexual offenders. The simple answer is no. Rapists fall into a number of different categories and each category, although inter-related, needs to be addressed independently. For example, the strategy most effective against the unarmed offender is generally not the strategy to employ in a confrontation with weapons. The stranger rapist must be handled in a totally different way to the acquaintance rapist. Likewise, the best way of dealing with the gang confrontation is in marked contrast to dealing with an individual offender.

By identifying a specific category or 'offender type' we can go on to identify common traits and typical patterns within that category. This in turn enables us not only to understand the offender, but to select the appropriate strategy to use against him.

The following is a sample of offenders from the 'serial stranger rapist' category I have studied and profiled over the past ten years.

Case study one

In 1992 I profiled an offender we will call Jerry Anderson. At the time he had just been convicted of a series of sexual assaults committed in NSW during 1991. He is currently serving a term of life imprisonment. Anderson is a very typical example of the serial stranger rapist.

Offender details

▪ Height: 170 cm

- Weight: 70 kg
- Age (at time of arrest): 21
- Single, living with parents

Case details

Over a period of 12 to 18 months Anderson attacked 12 women that we know of (bearing in mind most studies would agree that only one in ten sexual cases are reported to the police).

Anderson's selection process or 'method of operation' was the same in every case.

Each victim was aged between 18 and 35 years, living alone in a house that was poorly secured enough for Anderson to gain entry without being detected. The point of entry was usually an open window or an unlocked door. Each victim was attacked between 1.00 a.m. and 3.00 a.m.

Anderson would wear a black balaclava, dark T-shirt, jeans and a pair of runners.

Once inside the house, he would make his way to the victim's bedroom. He would grab the sleeping victim around the throat and start to choke her. Anderson would threaten the woman with physical violence in order to make her submit. He would then go on to rape and physically assault her, then threaten to return and kill her if she reported it to the police.

Anderson attacked 12 women in this fashion. However, not all of his selected victims were raped. Of the 12 women he selected ten were raped, beaten up and threatened with death and two were not. After his arrest

Anderson was asked why he selected twelve women but only went on to rape ten. This was his reply: *'Because two of them didn't do what they were supposed to do.'* What is it they were *supposed* to do exactly? Respond in the same way as the women did that Anderson went on to rape — submissively.

I am not being critical of the way the women who were raped responded. Every woman in this type of confrontation responds in a way which she believes is the best and safest for her at the time. My concern is what we as a society condition girls and women to *believe* is the best and safest way to respond to this type of confrontation.

All ten women who responded submissively, offering no physical or verbal defense to Anderson, were raped, beaten and threatened with death if they reported the rape to the police. The two women who responded by being physically and verbally aggressive toward Anderson were not raped, beaten or threatened with death. In fact Anderson *ran away from them both!*

The first of the women to fight back was Anderson's eighth victim. She screamed and physically lashed out at him, punching, scratching and kicking. Anderson pulled back, waited a few seconds, then ran from the house.

The second woman to fight back was his eleventh victim. She also responded by being verbally and physically aggressive when he attacked her. She also reported that Anderson ran from the house.

Can we say that every woman who fights back against this type of offender will get away? No, obviously that is not true. However, the more we understand about the mind-set and selection process of the offender the more likely we are to identify the most effective strategy to use against him.

This case highlights very clearly the fact that sexual offenders select victims they believe will offer little or no resistance. If things go according to plan the offender basically just carries out the fantasy of having power over his victims. However, if the response from the victim is one of assertiveness and aggression we can see, from this case, the offender is far less likely to proceed.

I have no doubt Anderson had the same intention with each of the 12 women that he selected. Each was selected in very similar circumstances. The *only* fundamental difference was how the women responded. This response appeared to determine the outcome of the confrontation.

As outlined in his personal details, Anderson was not a big man (approximately 170 cm tall and 70 kg), although he was often described by his victims as being taller and far more powerfully built. It is interesting to note that in a recent US study conducted in American prisons the average convicted rapist was 175 cm tall and weighed 72 kg. We need to be careful of assuming all rapists are big, powerful, dominant and threatening, as this mistaken belief can lead to thinking that the only option is submission. Anderson was a small, lightly built offender who was obviously terrified of confrontation. As with all sexual offenders of this type, he attempted to hide behind a veneer of strength, a veneer instantly destroyed by the two women who stood up to him.

Most of our conditioning about rapists comes from TV shows, videos and movies. Most of these come from America. Therefore, it may be interesting to profile an *actual* serial sex offender from the US to see if the Hollywood version is an accurate portrayal of the real thing.

Case study two

On 20 December 1988, in Cleveland, Ohio, a serial rapist by the name of Ronnie Shelton was arrested and subsequently charged with a total of 229 sexually-related offences. The offences were committed against 29 women between 1983 and 1988. Shelton received a 3198 year prison term, the longest sentence in Ohio history, and as a result Ronnie Shelton is one of the most infamous serial rapists in American history. This is how he operated.

Offender details

■ Height: 170 cm
■ Weight: 61 kg
■ Age (at time of arrest): 27
■ Single

Case details

On 3 April 1983 the first in a series of rapes was committed in Cleveland. The offender, labeled 'the West Side Rapist' by the media, went on to commit a further 29 reported rapes, prior to his arrest in 1988.

Shelton would select his victims in much the same manner as all serial rapists. He would go out at night and find women living alone in homes or units that he was able to gain entry to. He was also known to select women with children in the house and use the children as 'leverage' in his intimidation of the victim. On some occasions Shelton would threaten his victims with a knife, or claim to be in possession of one, in an attempt to frighten them into submission.

Shelton had a history of voyeurism (peeping and peering), from a young age as well as a history of dishonesty offences. The term 'dishonesty offence' refers to an offence relating to the theft of property, such as burglary. The link between this type of crime and rape is extremely strong as most serial sex offenders have previous criminal convictions for burglary/theft. When police are attempting to establish the identity of a serial sex offender they will often look at the criminal records of convicted burglars arrested in and around the area where the rapist is operating. This process often identifies the offender. In fact, Shelton was arrested or detained no less than 15 times by police in various suburbs of Cleveland during the course of their hunt for the West Side Rapist.

Shelton's method of operation was usually to watch his victim for a time through a window of their home. He would then gain entry to the house and confront them. Once he had made the victim submit he would rape or assault her. Before leaving Shelton would steal money from his victim and threaten to kill her if she informed the police. This pattern was followed for most of the 29 victims he selected.

This pattern of stealing from his victims eventually led to Shelton's downfall. In November 1988 he stole an ATM card from his last victim. After demanding the PIN he went to a local bank and withdrew money from the woman's account. Although he covered his face with a newspaper to avoid detection the security camera took a series of photos which showed Shelton's car parked directly behind him. The final shot shows Shelton returning to his vehicle. This was enough for the police to get an accurate description of the car. Shelton's vehicle was located in a restaurant car park some days later, and he was subsequently arrested.

Following his arrest Shelton was charged with a total of 229 offences and was later found guilty of 220, which included 49 rapes (he raped some of his victims more than once during the assault), 29 aggravated burglaries, 18 felonious assaults, 60 counts of gross sexual imposition, 12 kidnappings, 19 counts of intimidation, three counts of cutting telephone lines, two thefts and 27 aggravated robberies.

While in custody prior to his trial, Shelton was interviewed by Dr Michael Knowlan, a psychiatrist assigned by the Ohio Department of Public Prosecution to assess Shelton's sanity at the time he committed the crimes. Shelton made one particular comment that gives an insight into the mind-set of a serial rapist and it was included in James Neff's *The Pursuit and Capture of a Serial Rapist*.

Shelton actively searched out women living alone or in vulnerable circumstances with the express intention of confronting, intimidating and subsequently raping them.

But he did not rape all of the women he made contact with. This showed he employed some form of selection process.

During the interview Dr Knowlan asked Shelton if he ever had the opportunity to rape but had resisted. Shelton replied *'Yes, if a girl kept screaming or fought, I booked* [ran away]. *She was free.'*

So there it is. One of America's most notorious sexual offenders stated in an interview precisely what all those who study these types of offenders know beyond any doubt: they are afraid of confrontation. Shelton's selection process was based on the perception his victims would simply submit and offer little or no resistance, and he was usually right. However, if a woman was prepared to fight back and scream he would take off.

Like all offenders of this type, Ronnie Shelton lived most of his adult life in a self-created fantasy world where he constantly attempted to create an image of being tough, macho and aggressive. This image was an attempt to hide the *real* Ronnie who was forever compensating for his life-long perception of being inadequate physically, mentally and sexually. This 'compensatory' behaviour is highlighted in all major studies I have read on this type of offender, and will be outlined in more detail later in the chapter.

Ronnie Shelton continues to serve his 3198 year prison term.

Studying how people like Shelton think is very important. Their psychology may be repugnant to us, but the more we know about how they operate, the more we can use that knowledge against them.

A classic example of the police using their knowledge

of how criminals think to create a profile which helps them track down and stop a rapist is the infamous South Auckland serial rape case from New Zealand which concluded with the arrest of Joseph Thompson in 1995. He was charged with 129 sexually-related offences — more than any other individual had faced in any Commonwealth country.

Case study three

On the morning of Saturday, 15 July 1995, police arrested Joseph Thompson at his home in South Auckland, ending one of the longest-running police investigations in New Zealand's history. Thompson was subsequently charged and convicted of 129 sexually-related offences he had committed against 50 young girls and women over the 12 years between 1983 and 1994. He received the most severe penalty imposed in New Zealand since the abolition of capital punishment: 30 years' imprisonment with an order that he serve no fewer than 25 before his release could even be considered.

Offender details
- Height: 170 cm (approx.)
- Weight: 70 kg (approx.)
- Age (at time of arrest): 37
- Married

Case details
In 1983, at the age of 25, Thompson committed the first in what was to become a series of violent sexual crimes

against women in South Auckland.

Thompson's selection process was not unlike that of the two previous offenders I have outlined. He would walk around the streets of South Auckland, usually late at night, in search of women to rape. He would target homes that were poorly secured enough for him to gain entry, and once inside make contact with the victim. More than half of those selected by Thompson were schoolgirls under the age of 16. Once he had confronted the victim he would physically and/or verbally threaten and intimidate them to the point of submission before going on to rape or sexually abuse them. Thompson would threaten to return and in fact did so on three separate occasions, raping the girls for a second time.

During the course of the investigation the officer in charge, Detective Inspector Manning, used criminal profiling techniques to help identify and arrest the rapist.

Profile of the South Auckland rapist

This profile of the South Auckland rapist was put together before Thompson was identified as the offender. Its accuracy confirms how useful this form of offender analysis is.

■ The offender is a 'power reassurance' rapist. Compensating for feelings of insecurity and inadequacy; he has a need to express power, control, strength and authority through rape. This rapist type makes up 85 per cent of all stranger rapists and he is the most likely to develop into a serial offender.

Thompson was cateogorised as a power reassurance rapist.

■ The offender will fall into the category of a 'marauder' as opposed to a 'commuter' type. Rather than commuting to an area to commit his crime he travels on foot from a fixed location, normally his home. Over 80 per cent of serial rapists fit this model. These individuals generally live or are based close to the scene of the first crime in their series. They generally do not offend in an area immediately surrounding their home base, as this is an area where they may be well-known. Their crimes are invariably committed in environments in which they feel comfortable and which are well-known to them.

Thompson was a marauder. He lived within walking distance of most of his victims. As each group of rapes was categorized geographically it was found Thompson had in fact been living in each area when the rapes were committed.

■ The offender, being an intruder rapist (committing the rape after having broken into the home of the victim), will have a history of being a house burglar before he was a rapist.

Thompson was convicted of house burglary in 1977, 1984 (twice) and 1986 (twice).

■ The offender is unlikely to have a serious sex conviction prior to the first rape in his series.

Thompson had no previous sexual convictions prior to his arrest for the South Auckland rape series.

■ The offender is likely to have been first convicted of a

criminal offence at the age of 15. He is likely to be in his mid-twenties when he commits the first rape in his series.

Thompson was first arrested and charged at the age of 14 for burglary. He committed his first rape aged 25.

- The offender is unlikely to publicise his activity and is therefore unlikely to be nominated as a suspect by a member of the public.

  Thompson was seen by his workmates and those who knew him as very much a loner. In fact most believed him to be a fairly religious, quiet, family man. Even his wife, who was living with him most of the time he was committing the rapes, maintained she had absolutely no knowledge of her husband's nocturnal activities.

- The offender is likely to have been placed in a juvenile institution for criminal behaviour.

  Thompson was placed in an institution as a juvenile for theft and burglaries.

- The offender is likely to have exhibited criminal or deviant behaviour as a child which may not have come to police notice but may have been dealt with in an environment such as school.

  This is the only inference that was found to be inaccurate. No record exists of Thompson being referred to any organisation or service.

- The offender is likely to have been identified on a fingerprint trace at some time during his criminal career.

*A fingerprint left at a crime scene in 1985 identified
Thompson as the offender.*

Of the nine inferences drawn to establish the identity
of the South Auckland rapist eight were 100 per cent
accurate. This clearly illustrates that the various types
of offenders operate according to predictable patterns —
knowing this we can use their own psychology against
them.

As with all serial sex offenders I have studied, Thompson did not actually rape *all* women he selected, despite
the fact this was clearly his intention. I have summarised
six of his attacks, drawing on *Caught by His Past* in which
author Jan Corbett presents a detailed account of the
investigation into the South Auckland rape case. Having
interviewed most of Thompson's victims, Corbett was able
to outline the specific characteristics of each attack in the
series. It is this individual case analysis that clearly identifies Thompson's selection of his victims (whose names
have been changed) and responses to them.

1. Karen
   One of Thompson's series of attacks began with 15-
   year-old Karen, who lived in a single-storey unit with
   relatives. Karen was awoken at around 4 a.m. by
   noises outside as Thompson positioned an old table
   beneath a broken window of the house so he could gain
   entry. As Thompson came into her bedroom Karen lay
   terrified with her eyes shut. He held her down and
   punched her repeatedly around the head and face,

ripped an earring from her ear, and tied a petticoat around her neck. Karen started screaming at the top of her voice and her mother rushed in. Thompson then let the girl go and escaped through the bedroom window.

2. Grace

Thompson's next target was 16-year-old Grace, who he attacked in her bedroom as her sister slept in the same room. He punched her but Grace responded by screaming and physically attacking Thompson. She kneed him in the groin with as much force as she could muster and he fled.

3. Turia

Another one of Thompson's victims was 17-year-old Turia who he found asleep in a garage that had been converted into a bedroom. He woke Turia at around 6 a.m. by choking her. Turia grabbed hold of a knife she kept down the side of the mattress and lashed out with it, screaming. Thompson made a hasty retreat.

4. Ripeka

One of Thompson's youngest victims was 12-year-old Ripeka who he confronted as she slept in bed with her younger sister. He held his hand over her mouth and told her to be quiet or he would hurt her sister. As he attempted to get Ripeka to take her pants off she pushed him forcefully enough to make him fall from the bed and on to the floor. Thompson responded to this by punching her, but the young girl continued to resist and started screaming for her father who came running into the room. As he had done previously, Thompson escaped through the bedroom window.

5. Andrea

Thirty-one-year-old Andrea was awoken at around 3.30 a.m. by Thompson lying on top of her and kissing her on the lips. As she began to scream Thompson threatened her and started to punch her. Andrea fought on, screaming and kicking. Eventually she managed to break free and ran from the house screaming for help. Thompson disappeared in the opposite direction.

6. 'Jesus loves you!'

In another attack that wasn't reported to the police Thompson confessed to the police that he had broken into a house to find a woman alone. When he attempted to rape her she woke up. She frantically resisted him and kept yelling 'Jesus loves you'. Finding that he was unable to overcome her, Thompson ran from the house and disappeared up the road.

Of the 50 girls and women that we know Thompson selected, these six were the only ones not raped. Each of them screamed out for help and/or physically fought back. Can we assume therefore that *every* victim confronted by Thompson who screamed out and/or fought back was not raped? No; some of the remaining 44 girls and women did offer resistance but it was unsuccessful. However, the fact remains that each of the victims who was *not* raped by Thompson *resisted him verbally and / or physically.*

Thompson's selection process clearly illustrates his desire to choose women who would offer little or no resistance. Not only did he select those who were vulnerable due to where they lived and the time at which he confronted them, but as previously mentioned, his victims of choice were schoolgirls under the age of 16. These girls were not selected because Thompson was sexually attracted to them (rapists seldom, if ever, select their victims for this reason), but rather because of his belief that they would not offer any resistance.

The fact that each of the victims Thompson ran away from was yelling and screaming, and therefore drawing attention to his actions, confirms that he shared the most common fear of every sexual offender I have profiled — *getting caught!*

One final point about this case, which makes it typical, is the fact that Thompson invariably used violence against his victims *prior* to them resisting him. The popular myth that rapists only hurt those who fight back against them, is exactly that — a myth. Many of the victims most brutally attacked by Thompson and offenders of this type are those who offer little or no resistance during the confrontation. This aspect of rape psychology will be expanded later in the chapter.

Joseph Thompson, Jerry Anderson and Ronnie Shelton are all typical serial sex offenders sharing common traits and personality types which, when highlighted, reveal common weaknesses. It is through considering these weaknesses that effective response strategies can be chosen.

Serial sex offenders attempt to compensate for a lifelong perception of inadequacy through their crimes. They select victims they believe will offer little or no resistance. It is this low self-esteem, together with a desire to confront only those who will submit, which not only leads the rapist to commit a crime but also to flee when confronted or faced with the possibility of being caught.

This pattern applies, in varying degrees, to each of the many serial rapists I have studied. I won't outline them all, but here are some names you may recognise.

On 24 January 1989, in Florida, USA, Ted Bundy was executed for the murders of three young women. Prior to his execution Bundy admitted to killing at least 35 other young women throughout America. The actual number of women raped and/or murdered by Bundy is not known, but is believed to be far more than he admitted to. Of all the women confronted by Bundy the one that stands out is Carol DeRonch. She not only survived the attack, but went on to give evidence against him in court.

In her book, *The Stranger Beside Me,* Anne Rule, a personal acquaintance of Bundy, provides a detailed insight into the serial rapist/murderer, his crimes, victims and subsequent arrest. Carol DeRonch's case is the only one documented where the victim survived the attack. Rule outlines the confrontation:

> . . . In an instant he had clapped a handcuff on her
> right wrist. She fought him, kicking, screaming, as

he struggled to get the cuffs on her other wrist. He missed and managed only to get the second cuff on the same wrist. She continued to fight, scratching him, screaming at the top of her lungs . . . Now he had a crowbar of some kind in his hand, and he threw her up against the car. She threw up one hand and with the strength borne of desperation, managed to keep it away from her head. She kicked at his genitals and broke free. Running. She didn't see or care where. She had to get away from him.

Bundy's intention was undoubtedly to abduct, rape and murder Carol DeRonch as he had done and went on to do to all his other victims. Her mental and physical determination to resist saved her life.

Peter Sutcliffe, the man they called the Yorkshire Ripper, killed at least 13 women and violently attacked at least seven more with the intention of killing them. He was finally brought to justice on 22 May 1981, receiving a life sentence for his crimes. It was Sutcliffe's selection process, or rather how his selection process changed, that most clearly illustrates his desire to confront only 'easy' targets. Sutcliffe's first two victims were selected at random. Both victims survived the attack. It was at this time that he reassessed his selection process.

Investigative author David Yallop wrote of this change of victim selection in his highly acclaimed book *Deliver Us from Evil*:

> . . . It seemed to be the same in Halifax — even bigger, with ninety thousand people, but short on

unescorted women. He knew he had been lucky to find that one on her way home. Then she'd bloody well survived. Suddenly it came to him. It was so obvious that he was puzzled why the solution had taken so long to work out.

'Whores. Prostitutes. No need to stalk them, waiting for the right moment. Why, just pay your money and they come willingly with you, into the dark, into fields, alleyways, deserted areas.'

All Sutcliffe's remaining victims were either prostitutes, or women he mistakenly believed to be so. His selection process was simple — he only wanted those that came willingly, freely.

Serial sex offender, Albert DeSalvo (known as the Boston Strangler), was undoubtedly one of the first, if not the first, serial sex offender to authorise the writing of a book detailing his life, crimes and criminal profile. Gerold Frank's *The Boston Strangler* was first published in 1966 and serves as an official account of the crimes that occurred between 14 June, 1962, and 4 January, 1964.

Frank reported statements made by DeSalvo detailing his history of burglary, rape and finally the murders of 13 women. The following serves as confirmation, yet again, of the profile and mind-set of this type of offender.

. . . She turned and I had her. She was a strong girl, she fought, kicked, bit, and still I couldn't hit her. I could see her brown hair, dark brown hair, and when I turned and saw her face, I couldn't put my hand to hit her. I said, "I'm going to let you go," and I started to give up but she still had my finger in her mouth and I was doing everything to get her to open her mouth and she wouldn't.' He broke free. 'I ran out of the place grabbing my jacket from the chair, my hand was all bloody, boy she was screaming. She was really sounding off.

(statement made by DeSalvo during a police interview in 1966, from *The Boston Strangler*.)

This was an account of his attack on the only woman believed to have survived an encounter with DeSalvo during this time.

DeSalvo admitted to confronting and/or attacking literally hundreds of women during his lifetime and stated — *'Of all the women I attacked the only ones that were not raped were the ones who fought back'*.

Although Bundy, Sutcliffe, and DeSalvo had progressed to the stage of killing their victims to achieve their desire to have power over them, the same pattern of motivation, selection and response to retaliation is present as for less violent offenders.

Do *all* women who fight back against these types of offenders get away? Sadly, the answer is no. There is no one strategy that *guarantees* success in this, or any form of conflict. However I will say this. Every woman I have spoken with or researched over the past fifteen years who *has* escaped from a rapist has either *run to safety, yelled and screamed, or fought back.*

Having viewed the crime of rape from the perspective of the rapist, let's see what the experts have to say. We'll examine the findings of some of the most recognised and acclaimed studies of rape psychology and prevention to see what they have to say about the offenders and the greatest debate in women's self defence:

Submission versus fighting back

The American Justice Department, of which the FBI is a part, carried out a survey of one and a half million rape cases over ten years. The conclusions reached contradicted all previous assumptions. Researchers found that the injuries sustained by women who fought back were no different from those who did not. It was a myth that the risk of injury, be it mutilation or even death, was increased by resistance. It was also found that the women who used some form of self-defence more than doubled their chances of escape.

from *Taking Control* by Lynsey de Paul
& Clare McCormack, 1993

Without doubt the greatest debate surrounding women's self-defence is the question as to whether fighting back, be it verbally or physically, will increase or decrease the likelihood of being hurt.

To fully address this I'll separate the *type* of confrontation into two categories: the unarmed confrontation, which will be discussed for the remainder of this chapter and the confrontation with weapons which we will take up in Chapter Four.

One of the most common remarks made to me with regard to the work I do — and this usually comes from men, is — 'What's the point in teaching girls and women to fight back against a rapist? It'll only make it worse'. This statement is not only sexist, negative and defeatist, but factually incorrect. Every major independent study into rape avoidance compiled since 1975 agrees that an assertive, aggressive response to the unarmed sex offender is the safest and most effective option to adopt.

As I have continued to stress throughout this chapter, no strategy, technique or response is guaranteed to work in any given situation. However, the best strategy is the one that gives you the best chance and works better than the other options available to you.

I believe the options available in an unarmed rape confrontation are limited to *running, yelling and screaming, physically fighting back,* or *submitting*. Remember, the more knowledge you take into a situation the greater your chances are of getting out. The more options you have available, the less likely you are to 'freeze'.

In my experience the best and most effective option would be to run from the offender and if possible get yourself to a populated area. If you can't run, the next best option is to start yelling and screaming, not so much because some knight in shining armour will come galloping along and save you, but because the greatest fear of every rapist is *getting caught*. If yelling and screaming are not enough, I would advise physically fighting back.

Submission, in my opinion, is not only the worst option, but also the one most likely to result in rape and other physical harm. Rather than just taking my word for it, let us go back to what the offenders themselves have said about what works against them, and what the large-scale studies have found.

One excellent examination of rape avoidance is the book *Rape: The Misunderstood Crime,* 1993. Here authors Julie Allison and Lawrence Wrightson bring together some of the most current information available on this topic from a wide range of independent studies.

They focused on five major independent studies that detailed the effectiveness of self-protection strategies used by women who have actually been attacked.

The studies found that action was far more effective than inaction.

■ Sanders (1980) surveyed 481 women in Southern California, of whom 261 had been raped. After classifying the women's responses to assault into categories, he concluded that just about any form of resistance had some degree of effectiveness. In this survey the women who did nothing were more likely to be raped.

■ Queen's Bench Foundation study (1976) included 108 women, of whom 68 had been raped and 40 had resisted. The researchers found that women who avoided rape were more likely to use more types of resistance measures, to respond both physically and verbally, to be more suspicious and hostile, and to resist immediately.

McIntyre (1980) also found that women who were aggressive — and aggressive early — were more effective in avoiding rape. Hesitation in this study was associated with the likelihood that the rape would be completed.

Block and Skogan (1982) investigating 550 stranger rapes, also found that women who responded by physically attacking in return were less likely to be raped, whereas those who were less forceful were more likely to be raped.

Bart and O'Brien (1985) found that the more active the strategies used by the women, the more likely they were to avoid rape. In fact the more different strategies a woman used in addition to physical force, the more likely she was to avoid rape. They write 'We know that advice about how to behave when attacked, advice telling women to act in traditionally feminine ways, is wrong', and conclude that their best advice to avoid rape is 'Don't be a nice girl'.

Each of these studies points to the same conclusion: doing something is better than doing nothing.

The last study, by Bart and O'Brien, was taken from their internationally acclaimed book *Stopping Rape:*

Successful Survival Strategies, 1993, which the authors describe as 'a study of women who were attacked and avoided being raped'.

Their study, which is recognised as being one of the best of its kind ever conducted, is based on the analysis of 94 women, 51 of whom had been attacked and avoided being raped, and 43 who had been raped, in the two years prior to being interviewed.

Bart and O'Brien went on to mention other interesting findings from their study, such as:

> We are told that if we fight back, if we physically resist, we will pay the price of severe injury or death. Not only is this admonition not supported by our findings, it is also unsupported in the work of McIntyre (1980), Queen's Bench (1976), Sanders (1980), and Block and Skogan (1982).
>
> Furthermore, advising women to either comply or risk injury assumes that rape in itself does not result in injury, physical as well as mental.

> We know that women who resisted physically were more likely to avoid rape. But we also know that there was no relationship between the women's use of physical resistance and the rapist's use of additional physical force over and above the rape attempt.

These statements are very much in line with the comments I made earlier in this chapter with regard to Joseph Thompson's use of force, and the myth that if women fight back against their attacker they will be injured more than if they submit. The decision to submit is often based on this mistaken belief that resistance will result in increased violence and possibly death.

With regard to which *type* of resistance was most effective, Bart and O'Brien had this to say: 'Fleeing or trying to flee was the single most effective strategy that the women used'.

'Women who used physical force together with another technique increased their chances of avoiding rape. In fact, the more additional strategies they used, the greater their chances.'

'Yelling and screaming together with using force was the most effective *combination* to avoid rape.'

Avoiding rape

In summary, Bart and O'Brien concluded that they had identified four key factors in the actions taken by all of the women who avoided being raped:

1. Early recognition of danger. Be aware of your environment and constantly aware of any suspicious behaviour or individuals. Keep in touch with your instincts; they seldom lie.
2. A strong determination to resist being raped. Focus on what *you* can do to get out of the situation as opposed to focusing solely on what *he* is going to do to you. Be prepared to do whatever it takes to win.
3. Converting fear into anger. As we discussed back in Chapter One, this is a key to self-defence. Allow

yourself to get angry, I mean *really* angry that this loser has had the gall to select you! Use your anger to fuel your aggression and channel it against the offender.

4. An immediate and forceful response. All the evidence points towards the importance of immediate and force-ful resistance, whether it is running, screaming or fighting back.

The following excerpt from a letter sent to Professor Bart serves as a timely reminder, not only of the power of society's conditioning, but also how damaging that conditioning can be:

> 'Four months ago I was raped . . . Following conventional wisdom, I reacted to the attack calmly, nonviolently, and tried to talk my assailant out of it. To this day I feel worse about having cried and pleaded than I do about the sexual act.
>
> I hope that you will do a follow-up study on women who have been attacked [and who fought back]. I suspect you will find that even those that were ultimately raped have better feelings about themselves and are more easily readjusting to life. I am very grateful to be alive, and sometimes it seems even foolish to think this, but if there is a next time, they'll have to kill me.'

I estimate that I have spoken to well over 2500 women who have been raped. I asked the majority what they would do if they were ever in the situation again. Almost without exception they told me they would do whatever was necessary to get out of the situation: yell, scream, kick, punch, bite or even kill the guy if it meant avoiding rape. Sadly, many of these women had offered little or no resistance during their actual attack. It reflects poorly on our society that so many of these women had to actually go through a rape confrontation before identifying the 'conventional wisdom' of submission, begging and pleading for what it is — absolute crap!

The Behavioural Studies Unit of the FBI has, for a long time, been a reliable source of knowledge and statistical data in the area of criminal profiling and sexual assault. The book *Sexual Homicide: Patterns and Motives* was written by Robert Ressler, then supervisory special agent with the FBI, and creator of the FBI's criminal profiling system, Ann Burgess, then Professor of Psychiatric Mental Health, and John Douglas, then supervisory special agent with the FBI and program manager of the bureau's Criminal Profiling and Consultation Program. It presents a study of 108 convicted rapists and 389 of their victims on the correlation between victim responses and offender reactions to these responses.

Strategies to use

They summarised their recommended strategies thus:

Step 1. *Firm verbal confrontation.* Firmly tell the attacker to get away and leave you alone.

If Step 1 is unsuccessful:

Step 2. *Physical confrontation*. Immediately take the offensive and attack the assaulter with moderate physical aggression (hit, kick, punch, etc).

If Step 2 is unsuccessful:

Step 3. *Nonconfrontative verbal responses*. Attempt to calm the assaulter and talk him down from his rage. Engage him in conversation, and make yourself a real person to him. Challenge his fantasy that you are the person he wants to harm. Set the stage for an escape attempt.

If Step 3 is unsuccessful in neutralizing the violence:

Step 4. *Violent confrontation*. Use extreme aggression, and take any action within your means (kick, punch, bite, strike with rock, etc) to incapacitate the assaulter and avoid rape or mortal physical injury.

Ressler, Burgess and Douglas also say '*Knowledge* may be the only weapon a victim has in a highly dangerous situation. As such, knowledge can provide a sense of power, as well as the confidence necessary to *act* rather than resign out of helplessness.'

My only comment with regard to the abovementioned study would be that Step 3, nonconfrontative verbal responses, is more applicable to confronting an armed attacker than an unarmed offender and it will be expanded upon in the following chapter.

The overwhelming message in every one of the studies into rape avoidance is clear — *submission as a strategy doesn't work. Action is better than inaction.*

Here are a few additional studies I present in my seminars that may help dispel the myth that submission and passive resistance are the best strategies once and for all:

By far the majority of unarmed attackers are beaten off by women who *do* something. Eighty five per cent of women who yelled to attract attention, and resisted, escaped. If they responded in only one of these ways they still escaped over 50 per cent of the time. But women who did neither rarely escaped.

Victim Resistance Studies, Javorek and Selkin, study conducted with Denver General Hospital Crime Prevention Unit quoted in *Self-Protection for Women: A Seminar/Workshop Guide for Presenters* by Bronilyn Smith

Successful resistance is not so much a matter of using the 'best' method, as it is one of awareness and preparedness: For women to deter assault they must be alert and suspicious, and not be overwhelmed by fear and panic. They must focus on ways to get out of the situation, be determined not to be raped, be willing to risk and experience pain or injury, and present a firm resistance.

Self-defense: Steps to Success by Joan M. Nelson

A confident, assertive response to testing often deters the assailant because he can't be sure his intended victim will be easy to overpower and control. If his intended victim doesn't act like an 'easy victim' the assailant often prefers to back down and look for an easier victim.

'Using confrontation to deter sexual assault',
Dr Jayne Schultman

So the next time someone suggests to you that the safest thing to do in an unarmed rape confrontation is to lie back and submit, remember that they have absolutely no idea what they are talking about, and that you now have more than enough evidence and ammunition to actually prove it!

Now combine the knowledge gained from the offenders with that of the studies into rape avoidance.

A typical unarmed rape confrontation

Remember the many direct parallels between sexual harassment and sexual assault. Let us apply what we know about sexual harassment to a typical unarmed rape confrontation:

- The rapist will select a victim based on his perception that, due to circumstances such as the woman being alone, together with where and when he is attacking, she will offer little or no resistance and is therefore a good target.
- The rapist is compensating for a feeling of inadequacy and is looking for a submissive response to enable him to feel powerful.
- All evidence suggests that not only are sexual offenders looking for a submissive response from their victims, but that submission will result in the

confrontation continuing and the situation getting worse for the woman concerned.

■ Rape is the ultimate expression of male weakness, because sexual offenders are motivated by their life-long perception of weakness and inadequacy. Rape is merely a veneer of strength that the offender attempts to hide behind.

Now let's apply all this knowledge to actually dealing with an unarmed rape confrontation.

The confrontation

Imagine it's about 9.30 p.m. You are walking home alone from a friend's house (at least two out of three rapes in Australia and New Zealand are committed either in the home or within a few kilometres of home).

You are still about 15 minutes from home when you realise you are being followed. You start to walk a little faster, and glance back over your shoulder. Sure enough, back in the shadows, about 20 metres away, is the silhouette of a male figure who has also just increased the speed at which he is walking. Trying hard not to panic, you turn to your right and cross the street. The footsteps behind you are also crossing the street, and now getting closer. What do you do? Keep walking and hope for the best? Stop and wait for him to walk past? Just ignore the whole situation and tell yourself to stop being so paranoid? Or actually accept you may be in danger and do something constructive?

Obviously, the final option is the right one. If your gut feeling and intuition are telling you something is wrong, then one thing is for certain — something *is* wrong. Never ignore what is an instinctive reaction to being in danger.

So, having accepted you are being followed — what next?

In my experience this type of confrontation is unlikely to be anything other than sexually motivated. If this guy were going to rob you he'd have done it long ago. The offender who follows a lone woman at night is usually after more than just your wallet.

Now you know the *type* of offender you're dealing with, what is your best option?

First, if you're still not 100 per cent certain that this is in fact a confrontation about to happen (some people are harder to convince than others!), stop, turn around and look at him. You will soon be able to gauge from his body language whether he is interested in you or not. If he is, get the hell out of there.

In the last chapter I said the key to dealing effectively with any form of confrontation is your ability to 'get inside the head' of the person you're dealing with. It's time to ask yourself, *'why have I been selected?'* and *'what is he expecting me to do?'*

This guy has selected you because you're a woman, you're alone and, according to his view, you're in the wrong place at the wrong time. He expects you to be so terrified of him that you will submit and offer little or no resistance.

Remember the basic philosophy behind effective self-protection is not to focus on your opponent's strength and submit to it, but rather, identify his weaknesses and target those.

The greatest fear this type of offender has is getting caught. This is where your ability to use the *environment* of the confrontation comes into play. As in this example, sex offenders invariably select their victims in populated areas. This provides him with a range of targets together with the ability to disappear back into the surroundings. However, this also enables you to tap into the offender's fear of getting caught by turning the environment against him.

My suggestion, therefore, having confirmed you are in fact being followed, would be to run to a populated area as fast as you can and make as much noise as you can in the process. A 'populated area' could be anything from a nearby house to a street with shops and crowds, a passing car, anywhere where there may be people.

Please don't presume I'm naive enough to think anyone will come running to help: they may not. My point is rather the effect this response will have on the offender.

Bearing in mind, yet again, that a sex offender's greatest fear is getting caught and he is afraid of confrontation, how do you think he will respond to you sprinting up the driveway of a nearby house, banging on the front door and screaming at the top of your voice that someone's trying to rape you! Put yourself in his shoes. What would you do? Get the hell out of there would be my suggestion! Here we can see why running or fleeing from an offender is rated as the single most effective response to a rape confrontation.

If the person is following you in a vehicle approaching

you from behind, stop, turn around and walk back in the direction you have come from, remembering to keep a safe distance from the vehicle as you walk past it. This technique is very effective, as the offender has to reverse, do a U-turn, or get out of the car to maintain contact with you. Obviously each of these reactions telegraphs his intentions and getting to a populated area is now your priority.

But what if you can't run, or you do run, the offender chases you, and just like in the movies you end up in a dead-end alleyway with nowhere to go? Well, if running from the offender and getting to a populated are is not an option, you have two options left: *submit* or *confront*.

Picture yourself in this situation: back against the wall, offender coming towards you, with running no longer an option.

It's at this stage in my seminars I ask those there to imagine that they now slowly reach down and unzip the sports bag they are carrying, casually pull out a sawn-off shotgun, shove it right in the face of the offender and say 'Rape this!'

How do you think he would react to this type of response? I think he'd nearly wet himself, back away with his hands in the air and take off so fast you could smell the rubber burning on his sneakers.

So, if you've got a shotgun, use it. But for those of you who've left your shotgun at home you're back with those two options: *submit* or *confront*.

If we accept that the gun would work, then select the option that most closely represents it.

Cowering away, hands in the air, begging and pleading with the offender not to hurt you simply reinforces in his mind that he has made a good choice, and encourages him to continue. This is perhaps why begging, pleading and verbal stalling is recognised by all major studies as being the *least effective* strategy to adopt in this type of confrontation.

So if we agree submission will *not* work, then we are left with the second option: to confront. I am not suggesting that confronting will guarantee success, but if submission is your only other option, and that will fail miserably, what choice do you have?

Imagine, rather than doing what the offender actually wants you to do, that you respond assertively and aggressively towards him. You stand strong in an aggressive, fighting stance, arms extended, hands at the ready, feet apart, legs bent at the knee. Looking the offender straight in the eye you yell: 'BACK OFF! BACK OFF! BACK OFF!' As you move toward him ready to rip his arms and legs off if he so much as touches you! You've hit the switch, the 'bitch switch'! Now watch him run.

Your ability to confront this loser and get away from him has little, if anything, to do with what *he* believes you are capable of, and a lot to do with what *you* believe you are capable of!

How can I travel the country lecturing to thousands of women of all ages every year and tell them that this is the best strategy to adopt against the unarmed stranger rapist?

How can I dispute all those who suggest being passive and submissive is the best and safest option in this type of conflict?

And why will I continue to do it? I'll tell you why.

- Because in 1992 Jerry Anderson said the reason he didn't rape all of the women he selected was because 'Some of them didn't do what they were supposed to do.' Some of them fought back.

- In 1989 Ronnie Shelton, when asked why it was that not all of his victims were raped by him, said, 'If a girl kept screaming or fought, I booked (sic). She was free.'

- In 1995 Joseph Thompson selected schoolgirls as targets because they were less likely to fight back or put up any resistance.

At this stage I don't wish to go into *how* to best physically confront the offender if you choose to do so. A full rundown of effective defensive strikes will be outlined in Chapter Seven. The aim of this chapter has been to present an objective insight into the psychology of the stranger rapist, together with independent advice as to which strategy, or strategies, work best against them.

I often say during my seminars that the physical aspect of self-defence is the easy part. The hardest part is having sufficient knowledge and information to be able to reject the negative conditioning which promotes submission and passivity, in favour of deciding to be assertive, fighting back and claiming the right to say 'NO'. Once you know this is the most effective choice fighting back becomes an easier choice to make.

Summary

The message is simple. If you can run, run. If running is not an option, verbally confront the offender. If verbal confrontation is not enough, get physical. Be prepared to do whatever is within your power to get to safety.

This message is not only supported by all the offenders I have profiled, and all the studies I have researched, but most importantly, by the *real* experts: the hundreds of women I have spoken to over the years who have been successful in getting out of a potential rape confrontation.

Without doubt one of the most rewarding aspects of conducting seminars on women's self-protection is being constantly invited back to schools, universities and corporations to conduct follow-up courses for girls and women who have attended one of my lectures.

Rewarding, because in almost every follow-up course I have ever conducted I meet women who have actually used the strategies I taught them and been able to get out of potentially volatile situations.

I will always remember a rape investigation I was involved with when I was in the police during the mid-eighties. Not only was the offender a guy I went through high school with, but also he was one of the first sexual offenders I dealt with as a police officer.

I often think back to a comment he made during the interview with regard to what was going through his mind leading up to committing a rape. He said 'It's like a movie reel going around inside my head. It's like I've stepped out of myself and I'm watching myself in this movie. I'm playing the part of the rapist, and the woman is playing the part of the victim. As I grab her she's too terrified to do anything: it's like I've written a script for her. The script is like she's so frightened of me that she just freezes; she does nothing and I can just do whatever I like. Yeah, it's just like I'm in a movie.'

If ever, God forbid, you find yourself being confronted by this type of offender, remember he has written a script for you. But also remember, you have a choice. Follow the script, or rip it up and shove it in his face — the choice is yours.

4

THE CONFRONTATION WITH WEAPONS

We've looked at unarmed rape confrontation and examined appropriate strategies to deal with it, but what about armed confrontations? A question I am commonly asked is 'What if the guy has a knife?'

In Australia it is estimated less than 8 per cent of *reported* rapes involve a weapon. (*Without Consent: Confronting Adult Sexual Violence.* 1993). The likelihood, therefore, of being confronted by an armed rapist is not great but it does need to be addressed. It's important, too, to dispel the myths surrounding this type of confrontation.

The most common weapon used in a rape confrontation is a knife so this chapter will focus mainly on the knife-wielding offender, but the advice is basically the same whatever the weapon involved.

At this early stage let me make the distinction between dealing with an attempted rape/abduction and a mugging/robbery confrontation: if the armed offender confronts you and his demands relate to material items such as money, jewellery, wallet or handbag etc, then my advice is simple: hand it over!

Many such armed robberies are committed by offenders dependent on drugs (especially in and around larger cities), who have little or no concern for your physical wellbeing and may well be prepared to fatally injure you in order to get what they're after. No material item is worth the risk of being stabbed or losing your life.

A golden rule to remember in this type of confrontation is '*Never challenge the offender to use the weapon*'.

I was reminded of this adage recently when I heard of an incident at an ATM located in an inner city suburb:

A middle-aged man had just withdrawn $40 from his account. As he turned to walk away, still holding the money, a young man confronted him, brandishing a large knife in his right hand. The offender demanded the money.

At this stage I believe the guy with the money had two options: hand the money over and cut his losses, or be a 'hero', refuse the request, and see what happened next.

Well, regrettably, he chose the latter option and refused to part with his money, thus challenging the offender to carry out his threat. In doing so he broke the golden rule. I liken this to the tossing of a coin: heads, the offender changes his mind and runs off, or tails he stabs you *and* takes the money!

On this occasion, the coin came up tails: the offender stepped forward and stabbed the victim, who collapsed.

The offender ran off, stuffing the $40 into his back pocket.

When selecting a strategy always be mindful of the *end result*.

But what if the demands of the offender do not relate to material items. What if it is *you* he wishes to take possession of?

What if his motive is rape?

Is there a strategy that can deal with this, the most frightening of all confrontations? Thankfully, the answer is yes. There is a commonsense, realistic and effective method of dealing with the knife-carrying rapist. Of course, dealing with this type of confrontation is difficult and does not come with any guarantees. But there is a proven strategy which can help.

Let's see how such a confrontation unfolds.

The weapon-rape confrontation

The first step in addressing the weapon-rape confrontation is to dispel a few of the popular myths that seem to crop up every time this topic is raised.

The often-used media phrase 'Woman raped at knife-point!' is, in my opinion, grossly incorrect. In all the time I have spent working in this area I cannot recall a single situation where a woman was actually *raped* at knife-point. That's not to say I haven't spoken with women who have been confronted by a knife-carrying rapist; I have, on many occasions. My point is, that in all the cases I can recall, the offender was no longer in possession of the knife at the time of the actual rape.

I am not saying that women are *never* raped at knife-point, but rather that in the overwhelming majority of cases, the knife is used to achieve submission and once this is achieved, the weapon is usually put down. This is supported by the Australian Bureau of Justice Statistics Special Report, 1986, which found that in assaults involving assailants with knives, in only ten per cent of cases did the assailant use the knife to injure their victim.

Of course, this means there are some cases when the offender does keep the weapon at hand throughout the confrontation. Accordingly this situation will be dealt with later in the chapter. However, the knife is more commonly used at the point of contact as a means to intimidate the victim.

The reason *why* a rapist has a knife may not initially seem as important as the fact that he *has* one, but I assure you it becomes extremely important as we look at selecting a strategy.

The common perception that the weapon-carrying rapist comes from the psychopathic end of the offender spectrum and his intention is to chop you up into little pieces is also incorrect.

More often than not the rapist who chooses to take a weapon into the confrontation is one who believes that without it he will be unable to make the victim submit. A rapist who relies on a knife in this way does so because he needs to hide behind it to bolster his courage. This type of offender is clearly afraid of confrontation and resistance.

The belief that once you are confronted by an armed rapist your only option is submission is not only incorrect, but totally ignores one of the major keys to dealing with this type of confrontation: *Conflict situations never remain static.*

The weapon confrontation goes through a series of stages, as does the mind-set of the offender. If you face such a situation escape may appear impossible at the point of contact, but the situation *will* change. It is your ability to identify these changes and act accordingly that holds the key to your success. Remember, the offender has a script. The better you know it the better you'll be able to control the situation.

Now we've got some of the urban myths out of the way, let's concentrate on the typical aspects of a weapon-rape confrontation.

As with all forms of conflict, dealing with this type of situation requires an understanding of what is going on inside the head of the offender.

The first issue to address is the actual *purpose* behind the offender bringing the knife into the confrontation in the first place, and this is not so much to cause physical harm but rather to *intimidate* the victim into a state of submission. Once submission is achieved the offender's reliance on the knife lessens.

Stages of a rape

There are three stages in any rape: selection, intimidation and sexual assault. By looking at each one of these stages we can further assess the purpose behind a rapist carrying a knife.

Selection

The selection process of the armed rapist is the same as his unarmed counterpart. The offender looks for a victim whom he believes is vulnerable and likely to offer little or no resistance. *The weapon plays no part in the selection process.*

Intimidation

Once a victim has been selected the offender makes physical contact with her. It is at this 'point of contact' that the offender will attempt to intimidate the victim, both physically and verbally. It is during this 'intimidation' stage that the offender places the greatest reliance on the weapon. Intimidation leads to submission. Only when submission is achieved is the offender able to move onto the third and final stage of the conflict: sexual assault.

Sexual assault

This is the obvious intention behind this type of confrontation. I firmly believe that once the offender *perceives* he is in a position of power and control, and the victim has submitted, he begins to place less reliance on the knife. I often refer to this as a 'pressure cooker' situation. The pressure is at its highest at the point of contact and throughout the stage of intimidation. It begins to decrease as the offender feels he has control and starts to relax. Once the offender starts to relax, so too does his reliance on the weapon. It is this process that leads to the majority of armed offenders putting the weapon down *before* committing the rape.

The weapon-rape situation

Let us now consider how a typical weapon-rape situation unfolds (bearing in mind no two situations are ever exactly the same, the following example will outline a typical situation).

Point of contact

It is at the point of contact that the offender is most likely to produce the weapon. At this early stage of the confrontation the offender is most nervous and has the greatest reliance on the knife.

For the purpose of the exercise let's imagine a woman is alone in her house. It's early in the evening. She may be sitting in front of the TV, or perhaps quietly reading a book.

Outside, lurking in the shadows, is a sex offender, armed with a knife, who has just selected her as his next victim.

He gains entry to the house via an open window in the bathroom, and then quietly makes his way down the hallway to the lounge room.

Approaching his unsuspecting victim from behind, he grabs her around the shoulders and places the blade of the knife against her throat. She's told, 'Shut-up and don't move or I'll kill you'.

Now what?

Having found yourself in this type of situation the obvious question is 'What the hell do I do now?'

The simple answer is, at this stage: *do nothing*.

My advice to anyone in this situation is, at this stage,

to basically *do whatever the offender is telling you to do*. I would strongly advise against attempting to try any type of *active* strategy in the early stages of a weapon confrontation.

The only exception to this rule would be if you were faced with a potential abduction situation where the offender was attempting to get you into a vehicle and take you to another location. This situation may require more immediate action, as the abduction will undoubtedly lead to you being taken to a location far more advantageous to the offender than to you. In this case the *best* time to attempt escape may well be at the point of contact (and for more on that see the story on page 128). However, unless circumstances dictate otherwise, the early stages of a weapon confrontation should be used to calm the offender down as much as possible rather than confronting him and thereby increasing the likelihood of him using the weapon.

I call this process a 'submissive strategy'. The more the armed offender feels he has power and control the sooner he will lessen his reliance on the weapon. This approach is in stark contrast to the unarmed rape confrontation, but it needs to be if we are to encourage the offender to put the weapon down. This tactic is used by police to de-escalate armed confrontations.

So, in the initial stages of a weapon-rape confrontation I would advise staying as calm as possible, doing as the offender asks, and allowing him to believe he is gaining power and control over both you and the situation. Any attempt to confront the offender, unless absolutely necessary, should be avoided as this could escalate an already volatile situation.

When discussing the weapon confrontation in my seminars many women mention how terrifying it would be to experience this scenario. I totally accept this is indeed a frightening situation, but what makes this and other forms of conflict so terrifying is actually *not knowing* what to do. Once you understand the conflict, and have an effective strategy, your fear will decrease.

Remember, there's another person in the situation just as nervous, if not more so, than you: the bloke hanging off the end of the knife!

Once the offender believes he has control over the victim his next priority is to gain control over the environment.

Securing the environment

Bearing in mind that in this instance our offender has entered a strange environment to commit his crime (thus being an 'intruder rapist' as mentioned in the previous chapter), he must ensure the environment is secure as soon as possible.

Having gained control of his victim, this now becomes his next concern.

This process will often involve the offender taking the victim at knifepoint around the environment, in this case the lounge room, to shut doors, close windows, pull curtains and anything else he feels necessary to prevent detection. The extent of this would depend on the size of the specific environment/house. This aggressive action is often coupled with continued verbal threats against the woman in an attempt to gain total dominance.

Having spoken to numerous women who have experienced this I can say that not only is it terrifying, but also a point where many women mentally shut down, feeling that the rape is inevitable and escape impossible.

I understand this process and appreciate how hopeless the situation appears to be *at this stage,* but as I mentioned earlier, the confrontation will not remain static. Circumstances will change, and often for the better.

Having secured both the victim and the environment it is most likely that the offender will return the woman to where he first made contact or nearby. It is at this stage I believe that the first of many minor cracks start to appear in his armour.

For a moment, put yourself inside the mind of the offender. The situation is going exactly as planned: accessible house, woman alone, taken at knifepoint, victim has submitted and environment is secure.

I think it's fair to assume that the offender will start to relax, if even slightly, at this stage. All sex offenders premeditate their crimes and envisage having power over their victims. The armed rapist is no different. However, he believes initially he has to have a weapon present to achieve his goal.

Once submission has been achieved the offender's focus moves from victim containment to sexual assault.

It is at this stage I believe the offender is most likely to mentally place less reliance on the weapon and therefore physically start to remove the weapon from the *focal point,* in this case usually the victim's throat.

This removal of the weapon is not done for the benefit of the victim, but rather to enable the offender to move onto the next phase of the confrontation.

Although this change in the weapon's position may be small in terms of distance, it is the change in the offender's mind-set that is of greater consequence. Any move of the weapon away from the focal point is an indication that the offender is becoming more confident and therefore more relaxed. This subtle change in proceedings provides an opportunity to swing the pendulum back in your favour.

As the weapon is moved from the focal point let's look at the next phase of the strategy.

Which option is best?

The first phase in a weapon confrontation provides few options other than complying with the offender's demands. However, once the offender's reliance on the weapon decreases your options increase. This in itself can present a dilemma in that the greater the options the greater the chance of selecting the wrong one!

With this in mind here are the most common options suggested by those attending my seminars when discussing this phase of the confrontation:

- Yell and scream for help.
- Strike out at a vulnerable area of the offender (usually the groin).
- Grab the offender's wrist and push the knife-carrying arm away.

■ Run for the door or any available exit.
■ Do nothing.
■ Talk calmly with the offender.

Out of these six options I would predict four may well result in you being stabbed, one would suggest you have given up and are no longer looking at escape as an option, and one would have a higher success rate than all the others combined.

The trick is selecting the *right* option and knowing how to use it to your advantage.

The best advice I can give in this situation was actually given to me many years ago as a recruit at the Police College in New Zealand. We were told that in any confrontations involving weapons, *before you select a strategy, think about what could happen if it fails. If by failing it will make the situation worse, don't select it.*

Of the six options listed above, four are *active* strategies that may well challenge or pressure the offender into using the weapon — don't select them. The option of doing nothing is too *passive* and does not allow you to take advantage of the offender's mistake. This leaves the final option which I would suggest is not only the safest, but the most likely to succeed: talk calmly with the offender.

Talking with the offender

Talking is the only *active* strategy that, if it fails, will not result in the situation getting worse. This certainly cannot be said for yelling, striking or grabbing at this stage, or prematurely running for the door. By talking, the *worst* thing that can happen is the offender telling you to shut up. If this were his reaction you would simply do as he says and by doing so *reinforce* his perception that he is in control. I would then attempt to talk with him again a couple of minutes later, perhaps using a slightly different approach. Your aim at this stage is to engage the offender in some basic dialogue. The more he talks the more you gain control.

Bear in mind that although the offender is slightly more relaxed than at the point of contact, he is still nervous and focusing on the victim. This is not the time to verbally or physically challenge him unless absolutely necessary. The success of such a challenge at this time is too small and the likelihood of injury too high.

Obviously, if an opportunity to escape safely presents itself, then take it. My point is, however, not to try to force the situation too early.

Having selected talking as the best strategy the sixty-four-thousand dollar question is 'what do you talk about?'

Topics of conversation

There are two proven topics of conversation to use when negotiating a weapon confrontation:

1. *Control*. Reinforce in the offender's mind that he is in control of the situation. The more you do this, the more he will relax. The more he relaxes the more likely he is to make further mistakes.

2. *Humanise the situation*. As early as possibly tell the offender your name. Humanise yourself in his eyes by becoming more than just a nameless victim. This process has been found to dramatically decrease the

likelihood of the offender physically harming or killing the victim.

Talking calmly at a time like this may seem a little unrealistic, but speak with anyone who has been in a hostage-type situation and they will tell you that you just do whatever you have to do in the situation. If talking is the best option, you talk!

Here are a couple of things to focus on when talking with an offender in this type of situation:

- Initially, avoid eye contact. Play the submissive role, eyes down so as not to confront or challenge the offender.
- Be aware of your body language. The offender will initially gauge more from how you *look* than from what you *say*. Your body language must be in sync with *what* you say and *how* you say it. Act 'passive' and 'submissive': arms raised, open palms and head down.
- Talk in a quiet, calm, controlled manner.
- Verbally reinforce the offender's belief that you are afraid and he is in control, e.g.:
  'Please don't hurt me. You can do whatever you want; just please don't hurt me; I can't get away from you; I'll do whatever you want; just tell me; you're in charge. Please just tell me what you want me to do.'
- Attempt to engage the offender in conversation. The topic is not important at this stage; what's more important is creating some form of communication.
- Use 'open-ended' questions and avoid 'closed' statements that do not invite an answer, e.g.:

'Please tell me: why me, I don't even know you; why do you want to do this to me?' Is far more constructive than: *'You hate women, don't you!'*

■ If you are able to establish some form of communication, just keep it going. Ask plenty of open-ended questions that require a response.

■ 'Humanise' the situation, e.g.:

'Look, you're probably not interested, but my name is Mary and I have never been so terrified in my life. I'll do whatever you want, I just want to stay alive — I've got two little children, Jane and Peter — please don't hurt their mother.'

■ Focus on the offender. Look for changes in his body language. Watch what he does with the weapon. Look for signs of him relaxing; you want him to *trust* you.

■ Keep talking. Keep talking.

Your whole focus throughout this phase of the confrontation is to *act out* the role the offender has prepared for you.

Your goal is to gently manoeuvre his mind-set to the point where he believes that he no longer needs the weapon to contain you.

You don't achieve this by statements such as 'Put the knife down — now!' Remember that the majority of these offenders have no intention of using the knife for anything more than intimidation.

Don't try to talk him out of raping you. Your focus is the weapon. Once that is out of the way you can get to safety.

A common criticism of this type of strategy is 'What if

it doesn't work? What if the guy doesn't let you talk, then what?'

The point here is, it may not work — but how will you know if you don't try? If the worst case scenario is that the offender doesn't allow you to talk then you haven't lost anything. He will probably still put the weapon down at some stage anyway. All we are trying to achieve here is some form of *control* over what the offender does. The more involved you are in the situation the more you can play it to your advantage.

I am often asked about the prospect of the offender gagging the victim or tying her up. In such a case the offender would usually have to put the weapon down in order to do this. At this point you are dealing with an unarmed offender who is no longer relying on the weapon to contain you. This may well provide you with the opportunity to escape. (see Escape, page 100). Obviously the prospect of being tied up is a daunting one, and once bound the likelihood of escape is minimal. I would strongly advise that if this is about to happen, to embrace any opportunity to escape before it can be done.

Never approach any situation, least of all a weapon confrontation, with the attitude that whatever you try will fail. You have to try something; so why not channel your energy into a strategy that has been proven to work?

Remember that the offender is nervous. Nervous people talk. Every second you spend talking with the offender is another second you're gaining control.

Now what?

Having successfully established a level of rapport with the offender, albeit a somewhat one-dimensional rapport, start to really focus on the weapon and his dependence on it. You want the offender to put the weapon down.

One point worthy of mention is that the offender will not put the weapon down for *your* benefit but *his*. He would much prefer to have two hands free when committing the sexual assault.

Presuming then that all is going to plan, the offender removes the weapon from beneath your chin, all the time warning you that if you move he'll hurt you, and slowly places it down beside him. You are now dealing with an unarmed offender.

I have presented this confrontation in a 'role play' format in my seminars hundreds of times. On each occasion I take a volunteer from the audience who plays the part of the 'victim' and I take on the role of the offender. When I get to the stage where the weapon is put down I always ask the 'victim' how she feels and what is she now focusing on. Everytime I do this I receive the same response. Every woman tells me she is feeling a lot better now the knife is out of my hand, and that, for the first time in the scenario, she is focusing on escaping and getting to safety.

This is a vital stage of the confrontation. The pendulum has swung back in favour of the woman. The one thing that every woman focuses on at this stage — escape — is the one thing the offender is no longer mentally prepared for.

The importance of this cannot be overstated. The whole emphasis of the confrontation has just shifted 180 degrees.

When the offender makes contact with the victim he is being *proactive*, that is he has a plan or strategy in place. The victim, however, is *reactive* to the offender at the point of contact, as she is forced to react and respond to the offender's actions, which puts her in a position of weakness.

By employing the 'submissive strategy' in the confrontation you not only lull the offender into a false sense of security, but also manoeuvre the situation to the point where *you* become proactive and *he* is reactive.

You are now mentally planning a strategy for your escape, a situation the offender no longer believes is an option.

If an opportunity to escape presents itself during a weapon confrontation it will invariably come *once the weapon has been put down*.

For all the pessimists who may be adamant that the offender will not make a mistake at this stage and therefore think escape is futile, let me remind them that the offender has already made no less than *seven* mistakes in a row since the point of contact. If I were a betting man I'd bet London to a brick he'll make another one. One more mistake by the offender and you're out the door!

The offender's mistakes

To highlight my point here are the seven mistakes the offender has made so far:

1. The offender starts to *drop his guard* once he believes he has control over the situation. The weapon is removed from the focal point (the throat).
2. Having dropped his guard, *he allows you to talk to him*. You, of course, talk in a way that reinforces his perception of power and control.
3. Having opened up a line of conversation and structured it accordingly, you now find that the offender *starts to talk to you*, even if briefly.
4. This dialogue, based around 'control' and 'humanising the situation', *further* (mistakenly) *convinces the offender he is in control*.
5. *The offender's body language shows he is starting to relax*. He is now placing less reliance on the weapon, and consequently moves the knife further away from your throat.
6. *The offender believes that the weapon is no longer required to contain the situation.*
7. *The weapon is put down*. The offender is no longer focusing on containment and intimidation, but rather sexual assault.

These mistakes add up to your chance for escape.

By mentally focusing on escape, if an opportunity presents itself you are in a position to take it. I can't *guarantee* that an opportunity will just leap out at you, but bear in mind you only need a split second to make a bolt for the door or window and get to safety.

Because the offender is now focusing on issues other than you taking off, together with you suddenly becoming *proactive* rather than *reactive*, it is at this stage of the confrontation that your chances of escape are highest. Look for an opening and be prepared to take it.

Circumstances enabling escape

Here are just some of the circumstances that may enable you to escape:

- The offender pulling down his trousers. (Have you ever tried chasing somebody with your pants around your ankles?)
- A noise that momentarily distracts the offender's attention, e.g. a passing car, ringing telephone, neighbour, dog barking, siren, etc.
- The offender moving around the room or house.
- You suggesting that you go to a 'more comfortable' location.
- Physically striking out at the offender. Once the weapon has been put down you are dealing with an unarmed offender so be prepared to physically attack him if it will enable you to escape.
- Confronting the offender with his own weapon.

Remember, once you start to *focus* on escaping you will be far more aware of situations such as these presenting themselves. A split second may be all you need.

Escape!

Only the individual in any given situation can accurately gauge if and when escape is a viable option.

Effective self-protection strategies are those that provide options in confrontational situations. The aim behind outlining the above strategies is to enable you to see how you can in fact create and identify available options even in the seemingly hopeless predicament of being confronted by an armed attacker.

Only by being aware of changes in your environment are you in a position to take advantage of those changes and turn them against the offender.

Assuming an opportunity to escape has presented itself and you choose to take it, my advice is simple: *give it everything you've got.*

Prior to actually physically bolting make sure your chosen escape route is in fact available (deadlocked doors can hinder even the best-laid plans). Don't restrict your mode of exit just to doors, either. Windows are often a better option and there are more of them.

Although it is an option, unless it is absolutely necessary, I wouldn't suggest going for the weapon (unless the weapon is a firearm, in which case it would be advisable to have it with you as you take off). Focusing on a weapon will take your attention away from the most important issue: putting as much distance as you can between you and the offender. I wouldn't be too concerned about the prospect of the offender picking up the knife and deftly throwing it at you. Unless he works part-time at the local circus I don't think you've got too much to worry about.

I am not one who subscribes to the belief that using an offender's weapon against him is more likely to result in harm to you, but at this stage your focus should be on escaping rather than confronting. However, if confronting the offender with his weapon — or any other — is necessary for your escape then you may need to consider it.

So with an escape route chosen if an opportunity to take it presents itself: go, go, go.

Run for all you're worth and yell and scream loud enough to wake the dead. Chances are you'll be at the door or window and out the other side before the offender has even realised what the hell is going on, let alone taken any steps to prevent you getting away. The key here is the element of surprise, combined with speed and noise. If you can't get out because all the doors and windows are deadlocked then just getting away from the offender, even for a short time, still enables you to scream for help. You need to evaluate your opportunities according to the situation you are in.

If you can escape from the house the likelihood of the offender giving chase in an attempt to re-capture you and continue his assault is, in my opinion, very low. The other thing this offender has in common with his unarmed counterpart is fear: fear of getting caught.

Put yourself in his shoes for a moment and evaluate your options:

1. Take off after the woman as she runs wildly up the street letting everybody within earshot know what you've been up to, then attempt to overpower her, keep her quiet and take her to a suitable location so you can pick up where you left off.

Or,

2. Get the hell out of there before you get caught.

I think the decision is a relatively easy one.

Obviously every situation is going to be different in some way, therefore each one needs to be dealt with according to its circumstances. However, I firmly believe that the basic principles outlined above are applicable to most weapon confrontations like this.

If adopting a submissive strategy based on communication and de-escalation is not possible you may be faced with the prospect of converting any available item within reach into a weapon to defend yourself. This last resort strategy will be expanded upon in Chapter Seven on physical self-defence.

Over the years I have spoken to many people who have been involved in weapon confrontations similar to the example outlined in this chapter. The knowledge they have shared together, with my own personal experience has enabled me to understand the dynamics of this type of confrontation and develop a strategy to deal with it.

Summary

In weapon confrontations no one strategy or approach will ever work 100 per cent of the time. However, those who have successfully escaped this type of situation, usually have several traits in common. These are their ability to stay calm, communicate with the offender, identify his mistakes and act upon them. If you do this you are then in a position to evaluate the most appropriate steps to take and put them into action — whether getting away or fighting.

In their studies on dealing with an armed rapist, authors Pauline Bart and Patricia O'Brien concluded by stating: 'Even under difficult circumstances some women were able to negotiate, but they had to pretend to go along with the rapist's immediate goal (indeed some of them *did* go along) and then watch for an opening . . . Our major finding is that saying no or flattering the rapist is not enough. As long as the rapist's immediate goal is reached, or he believes it will be reached, he might allow the woman some leeway by behaving like a "nice guy"' (*Stopping Rape: Successful Survival Strategies*).

Never underestimate the power of communication in a conflict situation, and conversely be cautious of over-estimating the ability of an armed offender to gain and maintain control. Remember that there is only one person more nervous than you are, and that's the idiot clutching the knife.

5

CONFRONTATIONS WITH GROUPS AND GANGS

A confrontation with a group or gang has specific dynamics that are different from those involved with the individual offender. Therefore the actions you would take in this situation are different.

The prospect of being confronted by one offender is daunting enough let alone having two, three, four or more to deal with. However, as with the weapon confrontation, dealing effectively with the group or gang is well within the capabilities of most people if they understand the psychology of the situation and are aware of the key factors required to de-escalate it and maintain control.

At a recent seminar I was again asked a question that is often put to me. The following exchange highlights one of the biggest hurdles you have to overcome when addressing this type of confrontation:

A woman who had been very positive about all other aspects of the course asked 'What's the point of fighting back in a situation when you are confronted by more than one offender?' I suggested that the point in fighting back was to consider what would happen to you if you *didn't* fight back. Having thought about this she said 'But I could never fight off four or five guys in a conflict situation', to which I replied 'Have you ever had to? Have you ever actually been in a situation where you were confronted by a group of guys and you *had* to fight back to save yourself?' At this point the young lady shrugged her shoulders, shook her head and said, 'No, of course not'. Treading cautiously at this stage, wanting to identify the *real* issue at stake, I asked 'If you've never actually been in this type of situation how do you know you don't have the ability to get out of it?' She responded the same way every one does. She said 'I just don't *believe* I could do it. I don't *believe* I could get out of this type of situation'.

I think this is the most common barrier people put up when considering themselves in a gang confrontation; they simply don't *believe* they have the ability to deal with it. The issue is not so much the group or gang, but rather the *belief* that you are going to fail no matter what. As discussed in Chapter One, this type of mind-set causes fear, which leads to panic and usually results in total submission.

I am not suggesting that the gang confrontation is an *easy* situation to deal with. No confrontation is, but to have any chance of success you must approach it with an open and positive mind-set.

If you focus solely on the gang plus the fact that you

are out-powered and outnumbered, naturally you start to become a little negative. If however, as with all the strategies I teach, we focus on their *weakness* and your *strength,* the situation becomes less daunting. And in case you were wondering, the young woman I mentioned earlier went on to have total belief in her ability to deal with a gang confrontation after we had discussed the situation and examined effective strategies to deal with it. The only thing that had changed was her attitude.

Like confronting an attacker with a weapon, being confronted by a group of offenders is a frightening prospect, and no one strategy will guarantee success, but by breaking the conflict down into stages and identifying your options you stand a far better chance of being able to protect yourself.

Let's consider the most common stages of group confrontations and which strategies are most likely to succeed.

The avoidable confrontation

First we'll look at the group confrontation you have the option to avoid.

This might seem ridiculous — after all who wouldn't avoid a potential gang confrontation if they had the chance? But actually many avoidable situations are escalated when people take the wrong options.

Picture yourself walking home alone. It's about 9.30 p.m. as you walk along a relatively busy road and make a left-hand turn into a quieter side street. As you enter the side street you immediately become aware of a group of five or six guys in their late teens gathered on the footpath approximately 30 to 40 metres ahead of you. You stop briefly to assess the situation at the same time as the group becomes aware of your presence. Their talking dies down as they look around to see what you're going to do next.

So here we have it, a potential group confrontation about to happen. What do you do? What are your options? Which option is best and which will make the situation worse? Is anything *really* likely to happen, or are you just over-reacting? What are these guys thinking and how will they react to what you do next?

All these questions, and possibly many more, will be racing through your mind if you ever find yourself in this type of predicament. The trick is to *already* know the answers before being in the situation. As with all forms of conflict, the knowledge you take into a situation is what determines your ability to get out of it.

One thing to be aware of is the common fear of *over-reacting*. Often when situations of this type are discussed I am asked 'But what if the group wasn't *really* going to do anything? What if you're just being paranoid?' The short answer to this question is that you will never be 100 per cent certain exactly *what* the group may or may not do, but I would much rather be guilty of advising people to over-react rather than do nothing and endure the consequences. Remember to stay in touch with your instincts. If the little voice is telling you something might be wrong, then it probably is.

Having accepted that a confrontation is about to happen you must now evaluate your options and decide which one to take.

Options

In my opinion this type of situation provides you with three options:

1. Stop, turn, and walk away from the group in the opposite direction.
2. Cross the street and continue walking in the same direction.
3. Stand tall, shoulders back, look confident and walk briskly towards the group.

Let's start with the *least* favourable and progress from there.

The third option, walking towards the group, is without doubt the worst option of the three, but is, surprisingly, the one most likely to be selected.

The most common reason given for selecting this option seems to be that if you turn and walk away the members of the group will come racing after you, therefore you are better off walking towards them and calling their bluff.

There is certainly a time and a place for 'calling the bluff' of an offender as we have already discussed in previous chapters. However, when faced with the prospect of a gang confrontation this is not the option I would suggest.

My argument would be that if a group of people were likely to run after you if you turned and walked away, what is this same group likely to do if you actually continue walking towards them and save them the effort of chasing you? I think the answer is fairly obvious.

Secondly, by walking towards the group not only do you take yourself physically closer, but also, in their minds, *you* are now creating a confrontation, not them.

The decision about whether to confront or not is now with the group, not you. They have the option of stopping you, or letting you pass. Therefore they now see you as challenging their authority and you have lost a degree of control in the situation.

Finally, any option that increases the likelihood of a confrontation should always be avoided. Your focus at this point is to de-escalate the situation as much as possible. If avoidance is an option, always take it.

The next option I would strike off the list is the second one, crossing the road and walking down the other side.

Although this is a better option than walking towards the group I don't see it as being as safe or effective as turning and walking away.

It's a little like having a dollar each way. It may not be the worst thing to do, but it certainly isn't the best. If crossing the road seems necessary then surely turning around and walking away from the group is a safer, more appropriate choice.

Obviously, in my opinion, the first option, to stop, turn, and walk away, is the best and safest one.

In all the years I have been working in this area I have never heard of anybody being chased if they have taken this option when 30 to 40 metres away from the group. Groups such as these are not interested in blindly chasing after every person who happens to enter 'their' territory.

Ironically, this type of situation is in fact far more likely to escalate if you walk *towards* the group rather than *away* from them.

Think about it: if you turn and walk away and the group *does* actually start to come after you wouldn't you rather discover their intentions when you have 30 to 40 metres on them than when you're standing among them?

The key here is to be mindful of how the *group* is likely to react, and see the situation from their perspective.

Summary

Never underestimate how quickly a seemingly innocent situation such as walking towards a group of young guys can escalate and turn into an ugly confrontation. *If it's avoidable, avoid it.*

Sadly, situations like this are not always avoidable. Let's now deal with unavoidable confrontations and see how our options change.

The unavoidable confrontation

If avoiding the confrontation is no longer an option we need to find ways to de-escalate the situation and ultimately get to safety.

This scenario might arise, for instance, as a result of walking out of a subway straight into the midst of a group or gang, or turning into a street and being met by a group without having the opportunity to avoid them.

Having found yourself in this type of predicament there are a few well-tried rules which give you the greatest chance of getting to safety:

Do

- Realise that if you were surprised to see them, then they were more than likely surprised to see you.
- Remember *you* pose no threat to *them*. Attempt to keep the situation at this level.
- An individual always thinks faster than a group. If there are five, you think five times faster. If there are ten, you think ten times faster. This speed of thought is your greatest advantage. Use it by acting as quickly as you can.
- Your focus at the point of confrontation must be to de-escalate the situation and remove yourself from the most dangerous place in the world right now, which is where you are standing. The faster and more calmly you do this the greater the chance of getting away.
- *Act* fast, as you are thinking; don't think before you start acting. Physically remove yourself from where you are as quickly as possible. If possible, walk around the group and move off in the same direction.
- Ideally you want to be 20 to 30 metres past this group before they have time to realise what they *could've* done to you.

Don't

- Don't stop and stand in front of the group waiting for them to make a move. You think far quicker than they do and your focus (escape) is much clearer than theirs is. Use this to your advantage.

- Don't attempt to 'eyeball' any members of the group. As with the weapon confrontation, at this stage your focus should be on de-escalation. Avoid any actions that could be read as confrontational.

- At the point of confrontation don't turn and run away from the group (unless this will *definitely* enable you to get to a safer, more populated area). This course of action, although effective in the 'avoidable confrontation', is likely to encourage members of the group to chase you when they are in such close proximity.

- When attempting to move on past the group, don't try to muscle your way through the middle. Move quickly and confidently to the left or right and walk around them.

- Don't enter into any form of discussion with the group if it can be avoided. Even genuine attempts at communication can be turned against you in this situation.

- If you are successful in moving around the group and walking away, don't look back over your shoulder at them. This expression of fear may lead to a further confrontation. Focus on getting yourself away from them and, if possible, to a populated area.

Summary

Your focus in an unavoidable confrontation is to think and move quickly. Your greatest advantage is your speed of thought. The more distance you can put between you and the group, and the faster you do it, the better.

Of course even the best-laid plans and most effective of strategies cannot guarantee that this situation doesn't escalate into a full-on physical confrontation. Gang confrontations are by nature volatile and unpredictable at the best of times. With this in mind let's look into dealing with the gang confrontation that has progressed past the point of avoidance to where you are being surrounded and physically confronted.

The physical confrontation

Having attempted to move around the group and get to safety, let's presume your attempts have failed and you have found yourself surrounded by the group, with the prospect of simply walking to safety no longer an option.

This situation is potentially one of the most physically threatening confrontations you could ever be faced with. Taking the wrong option or pushing your luck too far too early can result in the situation escalating within seconds into an explosive, violent confrontation or abduction.

One of the dangers in confronting a group is the fact that the individual members of the group feel little or no responsibility for their actions. Each individual is spurred on by the actions of those around him. Peer pressure plays a major part in these situations, which can lead to individuals acting in a way that gives them kudos in the eyes of the group.

With the potentially explosive nature of this type of conflict in mind it is important to focus on a strategy that not only gives you a level of control, but also prevents the situation escalating to the point of physical confrontation.

Steps to take

I would strongly recommend these two steps be followed:

1. Identify the leader

This is the most important thing to do if the situation has reached the point of you being surrounded. Every group has one leader. This person makes the decisions for the group, therefore it is the leader who ultimately determines what happens to you.

As quickly as possible you should turn the group *confrontation* into a one-to-one *communication*. Attempting to deal with the *group* as a whole is a waste of time and will only increase their perception of power. Remember, it's not the group that decides your fate but the *leader* of the group. Address the leader, not the group.

Unless he's wearing a hat with 'I'm the leader', emblazoned across the front of it the leader may not be instantly identifiable. Look for the one verbally calling the shots or whose position and body language makes him stand out from the group. If you are still not sure, here is a foolproof method of identifying the group leader in a confrontation:

Approach the most likely member and say *'You're obviously the guy in charge here, right?'* If he is he'll tell you. If he isn't, one of two things will happen. He will either look straight at the guy who is, or the actual leader, not wanting to lose face, will instantly identify himself. Either way you've got what you're after — you're now talking to the right person.

Having identified the person who calls the shots, you have taken a large step in the right direction. In my experience, and while policing I had a great deal of experience of gangs, no other member of the group will make any move, verbal or physical, unless instructed to by the leader. Therefore, while he's talking to you, you have gained a level of control over the situation.

2. *Start communicating*
The best way to do this is simply to ask, '*What do you want?*' I know this sounds somewhat simplistic but *what* they actually want from you will determine the next step you take.

Your dialogue is now communication as opposed to confrontation. Physical confrontations with groups can generally be put into two categories: robberies or rape/abductions. The type of confrontation you are faced with will determine the strategy you adopt at this point.

The robbery

Let's presume that you are told the group wants your money.

You can now put in place an appropriate strategy. Although finding yourself the victim of a gang robbery is far from pleasant, it is certainly preferable to rape and abduction.

The obvious advantage is your ability to exchange money or material items for your safety. If dealt with correctly the gang robbery can be contained and your safety assured.

Steps to take

I would advise the following steps in this situation:

1. Keep a line of communication open with the leader of the group. Stand in front of him, but at a distance that is non-confronting. This is a potentially volatile situation that can turn nasty very quickly. Your focus is to de-escalate the situation and keep it calm and under control. This 'non-threatening' approach is in line with the 'submissive strategy' we discussed in the previous chapter.

2. Having told you he wants your money I believe the leader is actually saying. 'Give us your money and you can go'. The door to escape is now ajar; don't slam it shut by taking the wrong option. If it's your money they want, I suggest you give it to them.

   Nobody likes to hand over personal possessions under this sort of duress, but let's look at your options:

   a. Refuse to hand over what they want, thereby providing them with the excuse they need to attack you. Not only do you lose your money but you get beaten up for your trouble! *Or*

   b. Use your money as a means of getting yourself out of the situation as quickly and safely as possible.

   I think it goes without saying that the second option is better. Bear in mind that at this stage the group does not perceive you as a threat. This is very much to your advantage, as they have to *create* a reason to harm you. The advantage you have over a male in this situation, albeit a slight one, is the fact that the group is far less likely to physically harm you in a robbery if they get what they want. The same cannot be said if the victim were a male. When confronting a male the group needs little if any reason to attack. I'm not suggesting this is a *better* situation to be in if you're a woman, but attempting to highlight how best to use this situation to your advantage.

3. The act of handing over your wallet can be used to your advantage. There is very much a wrong way and a right way to part with it.

   a. *The wrong way* is to simply reach into your bag or back pocket, get the wallet out and hand it over to the leader of the group. This certainly gives them what *they* want but leaves *you* standing in a very precarious position in front of the group as they look through your wallet. This is an understandable mistake to make when your focus is on your own personal safety and you just want to do the right thing and not get hurt. However you have just missed a perfect opportunity to escape. You don't want to stay in this position for one second longer than you have to — every second you spend there increases the likelihood of your being harmed.

   b. *The right way* to part with your wallet is by using it to create a means for your escape. Tell the group, via the leader, that they can have your wallet and that all you want to do is to get home safely. Slowly remove your wallet from your bag or pocket, and while doing so *move from where you are standing*. You want to position yourself directly *between* the leader and whoever is standing beside him. This can be done by moving to your left or right. You have now created what I call a 'gate' between yourself and the remainder of the group. Don't be concerned about turning your back to some of the group members as long as you maintain contact with the leader. You're now at the 'perimeter' of the confrontation which makes getting to safety far easier than standing 'within' the confrontation.

4. Maintain contact with the leader. Remember, while you're talking with him you are controlling the rest of the group. Open up your wallet and tell him again that he can take it; all you want to do is get away.

5. As you place the wallet in the leader's hand step away from the group, turn and walk quickly but calmly to safety, putting as much distance between you and them as possible.

   The group will invariably be far more interested in the contents of your wallet than they are in you. As they look through the wallet (cash is generally the only thing they are after), you are getting yourself further and further away from them.

6. The way you *position* yourself as you hand the wallet over, together with focusing on escape rather than waiting for them to call the shots, can help you escape from a physcial confrontation.

   People often balk at the thought of actually handing

the wallet over so early, but as I mentioned earlier the alternatives are not too flash so why not actually *use* your wallet to your advantage? Presuming that in this situation the group will get your wallet *eventually*, I believe you must do your best to de-escalate the confrontation and spend the shortest time possible in such a dangerous situation.

7. An obvious concern, having lost personal items such as a wallet, driver's licence, credit cards, etc is that now the group may know who you are and where you live. In my experience it is extremely unlikely that in a confrontation of this nature the group is after anything other than cash. It is understandable to feel concerned about a group such as this being in possession of that sort of information but in reality I do not believe this creates any greater danger to you personally. Of coures you will cancel any credit cards as soon as possible and take every security precaution at home. Although this process is time-consuming and bloody infuriating, a robbery of this type seldom if ever results in any further contact between victim and gang. When they have the money the remaining contents of the wallet will usually be dumped.

Some years ago I was running a seminar when the topic of gang robbery came up. Although the seminar was for male employees, the basic principles behind the gang robbery remain the same. After I explained the best strategy to adopt in the situation, one of the guys in the course related a confrontation he had been involved in several months earlier.

While walking home from work he was confronted by four or five young guys who surrounded him and demanded his wallet. He did everything right with the exception of *how* he handed the wallet over to the group. He told us how he identified the leader, spoke directly with him, calmed the whole situation down, and agreed to give him the wallet. His only mistake was that he handed the wallet over and remained standing in the middle of the group. He then watched as they went through his wallet, took out all the cash and then threw the wallet and its remaining contents away. At this point the leader of the group stuffed the money into his pocket, looked around at his mates and said, 'Get into him, boys'. This was the only encouragement they needed. They all moved forward and attacked the poor bloke, punching and kicking him to the ground.

The fundamental mistake this guy made was waiting for the gang to make the next move. He told us that had he used the strategy we had just discussed (giving the money to the leader as he was stepping out of the confrontation and moving to safety) he had no doubt he would have avoided being beaten up. He said the group were initially uninterested in him and just wanted the money. It was only once they had what they wanted that they changed their focus from robbery to assault. Had he been 20 to 30 metres away from them at this stage the assault could have been avoided.

Summary

The key issues in a gang robbery are:
- De-escalate the confrontation as much as possible.
- Use your money or any other possessions to gain some form of leverage.
- Focus on removing yourself from the situation as quickly and safely as possible.

If this approach is unsuccessful I don't believe that you have lost anything by at least attempting it. The best strategy to adopt in this type of confrontation is one of de-escalation, which gives you room to move. If this approach is unsuccessful, then more drastic measures can be taken.

This leads to the situation where submission and negotiation no longer work. What about the gang confrontation where they aren't interested in your money, or your possessions, but rather it's *you* they want? What about finding yourself confronted with a potential gang rape?

The gang rape/abduction

In my experience the gang rape/abduction situation is potentially the most violent, life-threatening situation any woman could be confronted with and therefore the most terrifying to imagine. There is no easy way to address this scenario, just as there is no easy or 100 per cent successful way of dealing with it. Although not common, gang rape does occur and needs to be addressed accordingly.

As with all forms of conflict the gang rape/abduction provides you with options. Which option you take and how you take it can ultimately determine the outcome of this situation.

For the purpose of the exercise let's imagine this situation has started in the same way as the previous scenario. You do everything right: identify the leader, communicate with him, gain a level of control and focus on getting to safety. Unfortunately when you ask what it is that he wants you are told it's not your wallet they're after but you. The leader of the gang steps towards you and says. 'See that car over there, the boys are going to take you for a little drive and have some fun'.

The alarm bells start screaming inside your head. These guys want to rape you. No negotiation is going to be possible. What are your options? What are you going to do? Is there anything you *can* do?

In this situation you have two extremely different options available to you: *submit* or *confront*.

When you really get down to it, what other options are there? The big issue here comes down to what I keep reiterating. Your ability to get out of this situation is determined by your belief in your ability to do it. This requires motivation. The greatest motivation to confront this situation and, if necessary fight your way out is to think of the consequences if you don't: abduction and rape.

A gang is really nothing more than a group of weak individuals who feed off the perceived strength of their leader. As a group they are strong but as individuals they are cowardly and weak.

The prospect of having to physically fight your way out of a gang confrontation is a daunting one but must be compared to the likely consequences of submission. Also, the *way* in which you physically confront the group is paramount. Done the right way you can tap into the gang's weakest link and turn the situation to your advantage.

Cast your mind back to Mary, the woman I spoke about in Chapter One, who believed that she did not have the ability to defend herself in any type of physical confrontation. Remember that by using her daughter to motivate her, she turned this belief completely around. This same woman not only told me she would kill anyone who tried to harm her little girl but also demonstrated how she would do it! Do you think this motivation and determination to protect her daughter would have diminished had I told her that rather than just one offender there was actually four or five she had to confront? I guarantee it wouldn't. If anything her resolve would have become even stronger. Whatever the situation, what's important is your attitude and your belief in your ability to deal with it.

Having determined that submitting to this type of confrontation and offering no resistance will only lead to the gang achieving their goal, we must now focus on how to best fight your way to safety.

Fighting back
This is obviously a real 'back-to-the-wall' type of situation that requires appropriate resistance. Having been

informed of the gang's intention you only have a second or two in which to make a decision. Let's presume you have decided to take the only option that offers any chance of escape. You have decided to fight back.

When faced with the prospect of fighting your way out of this situation I believe the following points greatly enhance your likelihood of succeeding:

- *Attack the leader*. Any form of resistance should initially be directed at the leader of the group. When you flick the switch (the 'bitch switch') you must channel every ounce of energy, aggression, determination, and hatred toward the leader of the gang. His nose will smash just as easily as anybody else's will!

  By attacking the leader you immediately place doubt and hesitation in the minds of the other members. It is a myth to suggest that once the leader is confronted the others join in and support him. In my experience, the opposite is the case: by confronting the strongest you apply pressure to the weakest. Rather than stepping forward in support, most step back in hesitation.

- *Act quickly and decisively*. Don't fall into the trap of believing that if you fight back it will make the situation worse. This situation can only get worse if you do nothing. The most effective time and place to confront is now. If they get you into the car they will take you to a location which is to their advantage, not yours.

- *Don't try to negotiate*. This is not the time to hesitate or try to talk the gang out of what they intend to do. Your goal now is simply self-preservation. This could well be a life-threatening situation you are confronting and must be handled accordingly. Your focus is simply escape by whatever means necessary.

■ *Remember who you're dealing with*. As with all the offenders we have profiled, the individual members of a gang are afraid of getting caught. Most of them probably don't even want to be involved but are kept there by peer pressure. By yelling, screaming, punching, kicking, kneeing, biting and creating a scene you may provide them with the excuse they need to back off.

Remember that strong, assertive, aggressive resistance is likely to show this bunch of idiots for what they really are — a group of gutless, weak individuals feeding off the perceived strength of their leader.

■ *Be motivated*. Being confronted by four or five individuals simply means *you* have to be four or five times more motivated to succeed.

As with previous scenarios, actual physical strikes to use in this type of situation will be outlined in detail in a later chapter. But you now know what options are available and of those, which are most effective.

What if the gang is armed?

If a gang intent on abduction and/or rape are armed, your options are obviously reduced. Only the person in that actual situation would be able to accurately gauge the likely result of resisting. I am not suggesting that resistance is futile, but rather that the chances of success would have to be weighed up at the time, knowing the inevitable outcome if you submit.

Thankfully, in my experience it is extremely unusual for a confrontation like this to involve a weapon. I think this is because a group of guys would not consider it necessary to rely on a weapon to gain control over a female victim. I'm sure they would believe that their obvious advantage of numbers is more than enough to ensure success.

Group and gang confrontations always lead to heated debate in my seminars, and with good reason. For most people the prospect of having to confront one offender is bad enough, let alone four or five. Although I fully understand the concerns, the fact remains that if your back is against the wall you have only two options — confront or submit. Even if the better option doesn't appear particularly comforting, it is still the better option.

Let's hope if you ever find yourself facing a gang confrontation it will fall into either the 'avoidable' category or at worst the 'robbery' where you are able to use your possessions in exchange for your safety. However, if you find yourself in the abduction/rape scenario you must be prepared to fight back with absolute conviction and single-minded determination.

Amongst the most inspirational stories I have heard are from women who have escaped from this type of situation.

Recently I spoke at a secondary school. The students had all gone through one of my seminars the previous year and had invited me back for a follow-up course. At the end of the session I was approached by some students who'd had occasion to use some of my strategies during the 12 months since I'd last spoken to them.

One spoke of an incident she had been involved in some six months earlier. While walking home from a friend's place she became aware of a car cruising about 20 to 30 metres behind her. She looked back over her shoulder to see four young guys in the car who were obviously watching her. Before she had a chance to do anything the car accelerated up alongside her and two guys jumped out from the back, grabbed her, and started dragging her towards the car.

She told me it all happened so quickly that she barely had time to think and instinct just took over. She dropped to the ground and started to scream and kick out at the two guys holding her, making it as difficult as possible for them to get her to the car. She told me that one thing she remembered me saying in the course was that it is a physical impossibility for two people to get a person into the back of a car unless that person submits or is knocked unconscious. She wasn't about to submit, and she was fighting back so hard she was more likely to knock *these* guys unconscious rather than to being knocked out herself!

Once she was on the ground the guys grabbed hold of her by the ankles and continued to try to get her into the car. In desperation she grabbed hold of a nearby signpost and held on for dear life continuing to struggle and scream for all she was worth.

By now the driver of the car was getting very agitated

and nervous. She could hear him yelling at his mates, saying, 'It's not going to work, it's not going to work; just let her go and get in before some bastard catches us'.

Suddenly they let her go. The guys got back into the car and it sped off down the street.

Who knows what the intentions of that group were? All I know is that she beat them. The more she resisted the more nervous they became until finally the prospect of getting caught, combined with their inability to make her submit, made them give up.

Although it was a very frightening experience for her, in one way this girl was lucky, because she had the presence of mind to choose the most effective option and avoid being abducted and probably raped. But this is not always the case.

I will always remember a seminar I conducted around 1992. A young woman approached me as I was packing up my notes at the end of my presentation with a story initially the same as the one I have just outlined. But it ended quite differently.

This girl was also confronted by a carload of young guys but in this case they were successful in getting her into the car. They took her to a nearby field where she was repeatedly raped and beaten. This abduction occurred at 4.45 p.m. on a busy four-lane road in a middle-class suburb.

The effects of this violent, brutal sexual attack will be with this girl for life. She spoke of being too afraid to leave her house and return to school for over three months, of having to sleep in her parents' bedroom with the light on, and of shaking uncontrollably every time the phone rang or there was a knock at the door.

I met this girl six months after the attack. She told me how she was now feeling a lot stronger and rather than being afraid she was now angry. She then told me something I will always remember, and continue to use as motivation when speaking to women about this topic. She said 'I only have one wish whenever I find myself thinking about what happened to me. I wish I could wind back the clock. If I could, I would put myself back in that bus stop and wait for those bastards to come back. Then I would wait for them to try and get me into the car, and if they did I'd kill them. I'd kill every one of them.'

Sadly, this determination had arrived six months too late to prevent her being harmed.

I hope the knowledge you have gained from this chapter enables you to identify the most effective strategies for gang confrontations before rather than *after* the event.

Summary

If avoidance and de-escalation are no longer options and abduction/rape is imminent you must be prepared to physically attack the leader, act quickly and decisively, remember that a gang is a group of gutless individuals, and be single-mindedly focused on self-preservation.

6

DATE RAPE

So far we have discussed the unknown offender, whether armed or unarmed, alone or in a gang. While that's how most women visualise a sexual crime, in fact the most common form of such assault is committed by an offender who is known to the victim. All major studies have found that if the victim is aged between 15 and 25 years of age in 80 to 90 per cent of cases she will know her attacker.

The crime of 'acquaintance rape' has of course been around for as long as the more high-profile 'stranger rape'. However, it was not until the early 1980s that these two offences were recognised as being distinctly different in their psychology, although legally the same. Indeed the term 'date rape', which is now popularly used to describe this type of offence, originated in an article in the September 1982 issue of the American magazine *Ms*.

The purpose of this article was to create public awareness of the fact that most sexual crimes were not committed by faceless offenders in dark alleyways, but by men who were known to and trusted by the women they preyed upon. The overwhelming response to the article not only confirmed this fact but also led to the establishment of the '*Ms.* Project'. The government-funded project was the largest investigation ever undertaken on this subject, taking some three years and involving over 6000 students from 32 university campuses throughout the United States.

As a result of this type of public exposure and investigation 'date rape' has become a well-known term. Less well-known, however, are the actual legal definitions of this term, the mind-set of the offender who commits this crime and the strategies that are most effective against him. The following chapter will examine these less frequently discussed aspects of date rape.

But first I would like to dispel one of the great myths of the date rape debate.

Saying 'No'!

Nothing would please me more than to be able to inform the thousands of women I lecture to that in a potential date rape situation they could simply say 'No' and everything would be hunky-dory. That the word 'No', as if by magic, will send the offender running away with his tail between his legs, you will have regained total control over the situation and everybody will live happily ever after. But the fact of the matter is that saying 'No' does not stop a potential date rape from occurring.

Don't get me wrong. I'm not suggesting that a woman who is being pressured sexually by a guy she knows should not *try* saying 'No', but rather that you shouldn't expect it to work in every situation. Saying 'No' is extremely effective with a guy who respects you and is genuinely concerned about your wellbeing — but this guy is not the problem; he was never going to rape you in the first place.

My concern is the guy who *doesn't* respect you, who has little interest in what you do or don't want. *This* guy is the problem. This is the guy who made you believe he could be trusted. This is the guy who believes he is *entitled* to get what he wants. This is the guy who commits date rape. This is the guy to whom saying 'No' fails miserably. Remember, I am not condoning this in any way — just describing the reality of the situation in order to show you how to protect yourself from it.

Not only is saying 'No' totally inadequate in any date-rape situation, but all too often when it fails women don't know what to do next. This puts many women in a potentially dangerous predicament. I have spoken with a large number of women who have gone through this type of confrontation. Many of them believed that saying 'No' would give them control over the situation, only to find not only did it not work but in fact often made the situation worse.

As with all forms of conflict, in a date rape situation you must know what the offender is *thinking*, what he *expects* you to do, and how to *exploit* his weaknesses.

A lot of date-rape 'strategies' simply don't work as they

do not take into account the psychology of the offender. I recently came across a classic example of this in a book published in the late 1980s. Here is one of its 'ground breaking' suggestions for young women who find themselves in a date rape situation: '. . . You might try to do physical things to turn him off: urinate on the floor, pick your nose, belch, pass gas, even vomit — anything to break his perception that what is happening is a seduction.'

Well, there you go; no need to read any further. If you are unfortunate enough to find yourself in a date rape situation simply shove your fingers up your nose and voluntarily loose your bodily functions and you'll be safe.

Although I can't say that these somewhat bizarre techniques would definitely fail I believe you would be better served channelling your energies into a strategy more suited to exploiting the psychology of this type of offender. I am doubtful that simply putting your fingers up your nose or passing wind would be enough to have a potential date rapist running for the door. I agree to a point that anything is worth a go, but feel we can do a little better than this.

In the final stage of this chapter I will outline a strategy designed to get you out of most date rape situations. I have taught the strategy for many years and am confident that it works more effectively than any other that I know of.

But let's start by examining the legal definitions of this offence and take it from there.

Legal definitions

As already mentioned, the term 'date rape' is not a legal term but was coined by a journalist in 1982. In my experience most people do not know the legal definition of what we generally refer to as 'date rape'. This often means that women have difficulty identifying the offence that has been committed against them and it also means that men can believe that, in many cases, they haven't even committed an offence. I have lost count of the number of women who have approached me after a date rape seminar to tell me that last week, last month or last year they went through a date rape situation but didn't realize until attending the seminar that what they had experienced was a criminal offence.

Date rape versus stranger rape

One common misconception is that the *crime* of 'date rape' is different from that of 'stranger rape'. This often leads people (men in particular), to wrongly believe that there is one set of laws for the stranger, and one for the guy who knows the woman. If a guy went out tonight in the suburb where you live, waited in a park, pulled on a balaclava and raped a woman jogger who happened to be running past he would be charged with the same offence as a guy who invites his girlfriend over to watch videos and then has sex with her without consent. Both could end up in court, and, if found guilty, both could go to prison. Convicted sex offenders do not *always* receive custodial sentences. Under the law, if found guilty, an offender can be sent to prison but this is at the discretion of the judge as imprisonment is not mandatory. Having said this a convicted sex offender would consider himself very lucky to avoid going to prison. Legally there is absolutely no difference between committing a sexual offence against a total stranger or a person you know. Remember, 'date rape' and 'stranger rape' are terms that describe the *relationship* between the offender and the victim, not two separate criminal offences.

Defining 'date rape'

As straightforward as it may sound, the term 'date rape' is in fact somewhat ambiguous. When lecturing on this topic I often start the discussion by asking someone to define what 'date rape' actually means. I invariably get the same answers: 'Date rape means getting raped on a date, or being raped by a guy you know.' So what does 'rape' mean? 'Rape is when somebody has sex with you when you don't want them to.' So what does 'sex' mean when applied to the term 'rape'? 'Sex means intercourse.' So there you have it, 'date rape' is when a guy has *sexual intercourse* with a girl he knows without consent.

The problem here is that the term 'date rape' tends to exclude all forms of sexual contact *other* than intercourse. The term indicates to many women who are sexually abused by guys they know that if he didn't force intercourse upon them then it's not a date rape and therefore it's not an offence.

This is wrong. The term date rape covers *any* form of

sexual activity without consent with a man you know. If the sexual activity involves intercourse it is 'sexual assault', if it doesn't involve intercourse it is 'indecent assault'. Both are criminal offences and both carry substantial imprisonment terms.

Sexual assault

Note that, unless otherwise stated, for the purpose of illustration the information comes from the NSW Crimes Act 1900 (which is updated regularly). Each state and territory of Australia, and in fact every country within the Commonwealth including New Zealand, has its own version of the Crimes Act. Although the offences, the legal terms and definitions are basically the same there may be slight variations from state to state and country to country.

Sexual intercourse without consent is, of course, rape. However, the term 'rape' has largely been removed from all versions of the Crimes Act. It has been replaced by the term 'sexual assault'. The definition of sexual assault is the same as it was for rape: *'sexual intercourse without consent'*. Although the term 'sexual assault' is often used as a general expression to refer to any offence of a sexual nature, for the purpose of this analysis we will stick with the NSW Crimes Act definition that defines sexual assault as *intercourse* without consent.

So if a guy was to have sexual intercourse with a woman without her consent, whether she is a woman he knows or a total stranger, and she reported it, he would be charged with *sexual assault*, not rape. Sexual assault carries an imprisonment term of up to 14 years. In New Zealand the equivalent crimes carry terms of up to 20 years.

There are two other words that need to be further defined: 'intercourse' and 'consent'.

Intercourse

The definition of intercourse is far broader than most would think, as it does not *just* include penile penetration. The Crimes Act defines 'intercourse' as:

(a)   sexual connection occasioned by the penetration to any extent of the genitalia of a female person or the anus of any person by:

     (i)   any part of the body of another person; or

     (ii)   any object manipulated by another person, except where the penetration is carried out for proper medical purposes; or

(b)   sexual connection occasioned by the introduction of any part of the penis of a person into the mouth of another person; or

(c)   cunnilingus; or

(d)   the continuation of sexual intercourse as defined in paragraph (a), (b) or (c).

In other words, in the eyes of the law, what is *used* to penetrate the sexual area is not the issue, but rather the *act* of penetration without consent. A typical example is a guy and a girl in a car together having a kiss and a cuddle outside the girl's house after an evening out. Let's say the guy starts to go further than the girl is comfortable with. The girl makes it clear to him that she is uncomfortable and asks him to stop. The guy refuses to stop and starts to undo the girl's jeans. The girl repeatedly asks him to stop and tries unsuccessfully to push his hand away. The guy continues. He believes he is entitled to get a little more than what he's getting, and thinks that if he keeps at it the girl will eventually come round. As the girl attempts in vain to push him away the guy gets his hand down the front of her pants, thinking if he just 'touches her up a bit' everything will be okay. He starts to penetrate the girl sexually with one or two fingers. This guy has just committed sexual assault — an offence that could land him a major jail term.

Of course the majority of guys who have done this don't believe they have done anything wrong, let alone committed a criminal offence. However, my point at this stage is that many women who have been the victim of this type of assault are not aware that it constitutes a criminal act.

The act of penetration can also occur through clothing. If, for example, a guy forcibly penetrated a woman through her underwear using his fingers, this act would constitute sexual assault regardless of the presence of a thin piece of material between his fingers and the woman's vagina.

Consent

Like many legal terms the word 'consent' is often misunderstood. I think the most common misconception is that consent simply means saying 'yes'. Of course if this were the case no sex offender would go to prison because all they would have to do is get the victim to say 'yes' — whether they meant it or not — and whatever happened beyond that point would be 'consensual'.

In defining 'consent' the law makes little mention of *what* you say, but focuses more on *why* you said it: your own free will or some form of external pressure. It details a range of examples, from mistaken belief to threats and also absence of physical resistance. Butterworth's *Concise Australian Legal Dictionary* defines consent as: *'to give your permission freely, without the presence of threats, force, violence or manipulation'*.

The act of saying 'yes', or giving permission, does not in itself constitute consent unless such permission was given *freely*. Imagine a woman being pressured sexually by a guy and making it very clear that she wanted him to stop, and the man responds by becoming verbally and/or physically aggressive. If as a result of this aggression the woman becomes intimidated, frightened or concerned for her own safety and therefore starts to accede to the guy's demands, this is clearly not consent. It is submission.

It can be likened to a robbery. If you were confronted by a total stranger who demanded that you give him money or he would physically harm you, handing over your wallet is not consent but submission. The same principle applies to an unwanted sexual act.

Two other points made in the legal dictionary's definition of consent include:

■ that there should be *'an "affirmative" acceptance to the act in question, not merely an absence of objection.'* In other words, consent cannot be assumed.

that consent can only be given by a *'rational and sober person able to form a reasonable opinion upon the matter to which he or she consents.'*

Therefore it is unlawful to have sexual contact with a person who, due to the effects of drugs and/or alcohol, is incapable of reasonably consenting to the act.

If a person submits to sexual intercourse as a direct result of coercion or manipulation this is still unlawful sexual intercourse in Australia, and may be either sexual violation or inducing sexual connection by coercion in New Zealand. Inducing sexual connection by coercion applies in a situation where a person uses their position of power over an individual to coerce or manipulate them into submitting to sexual activity. For example, an employer pressuring an employee into having sexual intercourse under threat of losing her job if she did not agree. An offence of this nature carries an imprisonment term of up to six years in Australia and 14 years in New Zealand.

(Note: this type of activity would also constitute an offence under the Anti-discrimination and Sexual Harassment Acts under Australian state and federal law.)

Indecent assault: The 'other' form of date rape

Imagine a young woman at a party with a group of friends on a Saturday night. The party is beginning to wind down as people start to head home. A guy she has spent the evening with does the decent thing and offers her a lift home. The young woman feels comfortable about accepting the lift, as she believes the guy who is a 'friend of a friend' is trustworthy. She says goodnight to her friends and heads off to the car.

After a short drive they arrive outside the young woman's house. She chats briefly with the guy, thanks him for taking her home and suggests that maybe they catch up during the week. She turns to open the car door to get out and bang — his hand lands on her shoulder. She turns back toward the guy in surprise. The guy shrugs his shoulders, gestures down towards his groin and says, 'Come on, I gave you a lift home didn't I? How about you do something for me?' In an attempt to clear up this obvious misunderstanding the young woman says to the guy 'Yes, you did give me a lift home, and thanks very much, but if I knew that it meant having sex with you I would have walked home!' She turns around and for the second time attempts to get out of the car. Unfortunately the bloke in the driver's seat believes that he is more than justified in asking for something in return. Rather than cutting his losses, accepting that he may have misread the situation, and letting the young woman out of the car, he reaches across, grabs her by the shoulders and pulls her back in.

Here we have the classic 'Saturday night scenario' in which a young woman is about to be forced into some form of sexual activity by a guy who believes he is entitled to some sexual gratification due to the effort he has put in during the evening.

Holding the woman by the shoulders, the guy says 'Sorry, love, you're not going anywhere'. He then moves forward and starts to kiss her on the mouth, face and neck. The woman tries to pull away: 'No way! What's your problem?' The guy responds to this resistance by thinking 'Bloody hell; I've got a right one here', as he shoves his hand up the inside of her top, thinking 'They all like this; this'll bring her round'. The young woman keeps telling him to stop as she pulls his hand from inside her shirt. Unperturbed by this, the guy then pushes one hand down between the girl's legs over the top of her jeans while at the same time grabbing her hand and holding it against his groin. This situation continues for ten to fifteen minutes. The more the girl resists, the more persistent the guy becomes, all the time believing that he is doing nothing wrong: *he* doesn't have a problem; *she*'s the one with the bloody problem!

Let's say the young woman is able to break away from the guy before the situation progresses to the point where he forces her into having intercourse. She gets out of the car and runs inside. The guy drives off, thinking 'Well, that wasn't a complete waste of time; I copped a bit of a feel; something to tell the boys about tomorrow'. Meanwhile, the young woman is inside going through all those emotions experienced by someone who has just been sexually abused.

I have found that many women who have had this kind of experience are unable to identify what has happened to them. Also, out of more than 60,000 women I have lectured to on this subject since 1991, only four have been able to tell me the name of the offence that occurred in the car. What is even more disturbing is the fact that what has happened to this young woman in our story is the most common criminal offence committed against women aged between 15 and 25. This is the most common form of date rape, yet the women who experience it are often unable to name it, and most of the guys who commit it don't believe they're doing anything wrong!

Many women confuse this offence with sexual harassment. But as we saw in Chapter Two, 'sexual harassment' refers to offensive behaviour of a sexual nature that stems from verbal or *minor* physical contact that is unwelcome and unreciprocated. Quite clearly the offence committed in our example of the car scenario is of a far more serious nature, although it does not fall into the category of sexual assault, as intercourse did not take place.

Because they weren't 'raped' many women in this situation mistakenly believe that the guy hasn't committed a crime, and therefore what happened must somehow be their fault. This belief is often reinforced by the well-meaning comments of friends and family, such as: 'Well, at least he didn't rape you, so that's good' or 'Maybe you shouldn't have got in the car with him. You know what guys can be like after a couple of drinks'. Comments like these reinforce the myth that unless you are actually *raped* there is little if anything you can do about it. Any wonder many women blame themselves, and many guys don't think what they have done is a problem?

What occurred in our car scenario *is* a criminal offence. It is called indecent assault, and it is punishable by imprisonment.

Indecent assault covers any form of sexual activity

without consent that does not involve intercourse. The NSW Crimes Act, for instance, says: *'Any person who assaults another person and, at the time of, or immediately before or after, the assault, commits an act of indecency on or in the presence of the other person, is liable to imprisonment for five years'.* (In some states indecent assault may be included in the offence of sexual assault and in New Zealand it might be included in the offence of sexual violation but there's also a separate offence of indecent assault, with a maximum of seven years' imprisonment.)

The ingredients of indecent assault are very clearly present in the car scenario that we have been discussing. The young woman was clearly 'assaulted' by the guy and at the time of the assault he touched her sexually, which constitutes an act of indecency. If the situation had progressed to the point where the guy sexually *penetrated* the girl the offence would then be sexual assault.

Just a few more legal points about sexual offences:

- In Australia, if there is more than one offender involved, or if a weapon is used, or 'excessive force', or if the victim is under the age of 16, the offender(s) can be charged with *'aggravated sexual/indecent assault'*. This also applies where the victim is under the authority of the offender, or has a serious physical or intellectual disability. A sexual offence committed under *'aggravated'* circumstances carries a substantially higher imprisonment term. In New Zealand there is no one equivalent to the offence of 'aggravated sexual/indecent assault'. However, aggravating factors, such as use of weapons or the number of offences, may have an effect on the sentence imposed for sexual violation or indecent assault.

- The legal age of consent is 16. Therefore, it is unlawful for any person over the age of 16 to have sexual contact with a person under 16, even if this person 'consents'. The law does not recognise 'consent' as being legal when provided by a person under the age of 16. The only defence to this charge is if the offender can prove that under the circumstances it was reasonable to assume that the victim was in fact over the age of 16 (or in New Zealand if the offender is younger than the girl). However, this defence cannot be used if the victim is under 14 years of age in Australia or 12 in New Zealand.

- Although it is recognised that sexual crime is mainly committed by males, none of the sexual offences mentioned are 'gender-specific'. Women *can* be charged, and men and boys can also be victims (although usually of male offenders).

- An offender can be charged with 'attempting' to commit any offence in the Crimes Act. The sentence for an attempted crime in Australia is the same as had the crime actually been committed but this is not the case in New Zealand.

- There is no time limit to reporting sexual offences. You can report a sexual offence the day it happens, the next day, a month later, a year later or ten years later. Obviously, as with any offence, the earlier an offence is reported the easier it is to investigate but there is no *legal* time restriction to reporting sexual crime.

I hope this has clarified the definition of the term 'date rape' for you.

'Date rape drugs'

Few seminars go past without somebody asking something about so called 'date rape drugs'.

Rohypnol is perhaps the drug most often referred to as a 'date rape drug'. Although, in my experience, in Australia it is not common to hear of any *actual* incidents involving the drug there is no doubting the reputation it has. Having said this you could argue that, due to the nature of Rohypnol and its ilk, those who have been affected by it might well have no memory of the incident.

Rohypnol and another brand, Hypnodorm, both contain flunitrazepam, one of the group of prescription drugs that are used as sedatives. The most common medical application of flunitrazepam is in the treatment of insomnia. As with any drug of this nature it can be used maliciously. Also, although very hard to dissolve in water it is readily soluble in alcohol. This, plus the fact that it is colourless, odourless and tasteless and therefore undetectable, means that in a party or nightclub environment it can easily be administered to a person without their knowledge. Since November 1999 Rohypnol tablets have been coloured blue, making clear liquid turn blue and coloured liquid turn murky, improving detectability. However it might still be difficult to spot in a colourful cocktail or other mixed drink — or in a can. Also remember that other sedatives remain colourless.

The direct effects of imbibing a sedative in alcohol can be many and varied depending on a number of factors such as the amount of drug taken (just one 2 mg tablet can induce deep sedation), the amount of alcohol that has been consumed, the length of time the drug is in the body and the metabolism of the individual concerned. But the most common reaction to the drug, and of course the very reason it is used under such circumstances, is the onset of deep sedation and the subsequent inability to resist any unwanted sexual activity. Another common side-effect is temporary amnesia or memory impairment which prevents the victim from remembering what happened to them while under the influence of the drug.

A drug which causes deep sedation and memory loss, is soluble in alcohol and may be undetectable — no wonder it has become known as the 'date rape drug'!

The most commonly asked question about Rohypnol and its ilk is 'How do you know if it has been put in your drink if you can't taste it, see it or smell it?' The short answer is: you don't know. You will, however, become aware of it once it is in your system. A doctor has provided the following list of symptoms to look out for.

Effects of flunitrazepam

Having consumed alcohol be aware of:
- The onset of a feeling of tiredness or sleepiness.
- Dizziness, disorientation, confusion, instability on your feet, agitation or a change in your state of mind.
- Any unfamiliar reaction you would not usually

associate with drinking alcohol.

■ These reactions can occur within half an hour to two hours after taking the drug.

This depends on the amount of alcohol you have consumed — the greater the amount, the greater the effect of the drug. Also, although some of the symptoms are similar to those of being drunk, the symptoms associated with flunitrazepam are of a rapid onset half an hour to two hours after ingestion. So when the drug takes effect most people are aware of a rapid change in their mental and physical state as opposed to the more gradual effects of alcohol.

If you suspect that you or a friend has been given a sedative such as Rohypnol you should seek medical advice immediately. It has unpredictable side-effects, especially with alcohol.

The obvious danger of a drug of this nature is that you are totally unaware that you have taken it until it takes effect. This highlights the need to be cautious when in and around social environments where such a drug may be present. Be wary of accepting drinks from people you don't know and avoid leaving your drink unattended. Although it may be difficult to ultimately protect yourself against this type of situation a little bit of awareness and commonsense can go a long way.

If you can't get to medical assistance under your own steam, get to somewhere where there are people, preferably those you know and can trust. Tell them what may have happened and ask for medical attention.

Let's now examine the mind-set of the typical date rapist.

Beware the mind-set of justification

Understanding and effectively dealing with date rape means understanding and effectively dealing with the specific mind-set you are faced with in this type of situation. Although there is no legal difference between what we label 'date rape' and 'stranger rape', there is undoubtedly a vast psychological difference between the offenders in each category and each requires a completely different strategy.

In all the years I have been studying and lecturing on self-defence I have discovered one fundamental aspect that separates date rape from stranger rape: stranger rapists with the exception of pyschopathic offenders (a very small percentage), know that what they are doing is wrong and are terrified of getting caught. The date rapist has little if any concept that what he is doing is wrong, and his greatest fear is losing face through rejection.

Earlier we looked into the definition of 'indecent assault' in a scenario involving a girl and a guy in a car together following a party. The guy believed he wasn't doing anything wrong — a classic example of what I call the 'mind-set of justification'.

I well remember interviewing a young guy under arrest for the rape of a young woman he had met at a nightclub earlier in the evening. To my surprise he was quite happy to talk about the events of the evening, even to the point of admitting that he had had intercourse with the young woman in question when it was quite clear that she didn't want him to. In an attempt to defend his actions he told me he had been invited back to the woman's place, that he had been buying her drinks during the night and had even paid for the taxi. He added that they had already had sex once on the night in question and that about an hour later he wanted to do it again, but she wasn't too keen. He told me he knew she 'wasn't too keen' because she was yelling and screaming at him to stop and trying to push him off. I asked him what he did at this stage, to which he replied, that he held her down and had sex with her. When I asked if he could see the problem with that he said, 'Mate, I'd been buying her drinks all night; I paid for the bloody taxi; we'd already done it once. Yeah, she was saying "No", Come on mate they all say "No" what's the problem?'

The 'problem' was he had just admitted to committing sexual assault. The 'problem' was he ended up going to prison for it. The 'problem' was he didn't think he had done anything wrong.

This mind-set of justification is very important to understand and be aware of if ever you find yourself in a date rape situation. As was illustrated in our car scenario, the more the girl *resisted* the more the guy *persisted*.

The persistence of a guy in this situation is motivated by his belief that he is in some way justified in his actions. This is fuelled by his belief that he isn't doing anything wrong: he doesn't have a problem; she's the one with the problem. The more she resists him the more the little voice inside his head tells him 'She can't say "no" to me, I'm a good bloke. I bought her a couple of drinks, I've given her a lift home; what more does she want?' Of course through all this the poor woman just keeps saying 'No, no, no' because she's been told the more you say 'No' the quicker the guy will stop. It's just a shame no-one told the guy this. He thinks the more she says 'No' the harder he has to try to make her say 'Yes'. The harder he tries the more he justifies his actions: 'All girls say "No"; you don't listen to that bullshit. Come on, get into it; she owes it to you'. Beware the mind-set of justification.

Don't get me wrong: not all guys think like this. But the ones that do are not made to wear identifying tags when they go out to parties and nightclubs. Indeed, often the guys who pose the greatest threat are the hardest to identify.

Often date rape seems to be a real 'Venus and Mars' situation: the guy sees the situation from a totally different perspective to the woman. It's as if both parties are talking a different language: the more she says 'No' the more he thinks she means 'Yes'; the more she resists the more he persists; the more she tells him he's out of line the more he believes she's the one with the problem. A lot of this conflict is because this particular guy's conditioning and beliefs are often so different from those of the woman he is with.

Studies of male attitudes to date rape

All major studies of date rape have exposed this mind-set of 'justification' on the part of the guy. Here is just a typical sample of some of their findings, from *Rape: The Misunderstood Crime* (Allison & Wrightson):

▪ In a US high school survey 43 per cent of males

believed that it was acceptable for a man to force a woman to have sex if they had dated for a long time (Giarrusso, Johnson, Goodchilds & Zellman, 1979).

■ In the same survey more than half of the males also believed forcible sex to be justifiable (there's that word again), if the woman was 'leading the man on'.

■ Almost half of the males surveyed said it was acceptable for a man to force a woman to have sex if he had spent money on her (Giarrusso et al.).

■ The more money spent by a male on a date, the more he feels entitled to sexual intimacy (Korman & Leslie, 1982).

■ If the male drives, he is providing a 'service' that he may feel must be paid for. Symbolically, he may feel entitled to sex with his date (Muehlenhard & Linton, 1987).

■ Some men really do believe that women want sex even though they say no (Shotland & Goodstein, 1983). 'Sometimes a woman has to resist your advances to show how sincere she is. And so, sometimes you've gotta help them along. You know she means "No" the first time, but the third time she could say "No" all night and you know she doesn't mean it' (Sanday, 1990).

■ A male's persistence may increase because he may really believe that she is only engaging in 'token' resistance. Consistent with this notion is the fact that the most common strategy used by sexually coercive men involves merely ignoring the woman's pleas (Rapaport & Burkhart, 1984).

■ In one study more than 25 per cent of university men

reported that they had engaged in aggressive sexual activity with a woman even after she had responded to their attempts with either fighting, crying, screaming or pleading (Kanin, 1984).

- Another study by the same researcher (Kanin, 1984), using as subjects self-disclosed date rapists, found that two-thirds of them felt the fault of the incident rested with the woman.

- A woman's resistance is often not taken seriously. When a woman is honestly trying to resist a man's sexual advances, yet he believes she actually wants him to pursue the advances, it is the direct result of miscommunication and of perceiving the situation inaccurately (Johnson, Freshnock & Saal, 1993).

While these are American studies, per head of population, the sexual crime rate in America is almost identical to that here. Although a number of the studies quoted were completed some time ago I have no doubt that the attitudes and misconceptions mentioned are still very much present today. I conduct seminars for young men in a large number of schools and universities and whenever the topic of date rape is discussed I inevitably hear comments along the line of those in these studies.

Now that we know how the guy *thinks* we are a large step closer to selecting a strategy that *will* work against him.

Prior to outlining my date rape strategy there is just one more important issue that needs to be addressed: the issue of trust.

'He seemed like such a nice guy . . .'

If I had to identify one common denominator in every date rape situation that has been reported to me it would be 'trust', or more specifically, 'misplaced trust'. Almost without exception every woman I have spoken to who has experienced date rape has said 'He seemed like such a nice guy; it wasn't until we were on our own together that I realised I had made a mistake'. Another comment that is often made in hindsight is 'Looking back on the situation I can remember thinking that I was taking a bit of a risk leaving with the guy, but unfortunately I just ignored my gut feeling and went anyway'.

The whole issue of trust in these situations cannot be overstated. No woman would even contemplate leaving a party, bar or nightclub with a guy unless she thought that she could trust him. The problem is the guys know it as well! You don't have to look too hard to realise that if a guy knows that a girl or woman will only leave with him if she believes he can be *'trusted'*, he will simply act in a way that creates this impression. Add to this the fact that the guy's sole motivation to get the girl or woman on her own may be less than honourable, and it's not hard to see how these situations can turn nasty.

I'm not trying to suggest that *every* woman who leaves a party, bar or nightclub with a guy is automatically going to find herself in trouble, but if something untoward *is* going to happen it's unlikely to happen in front of a whole lot of people. I have often said in my seminars that these places are not dangerous in themselves; what makes them dangerous are the decisions that people make about who they leave with.

I'm frequently asked to describe this 'guy' who may be a danger. The problem is I can't; he is too good at disguising himself, (remember up to 90 per cent of young women who are sexually abused are abused by a guy they know, and more than likely believed that they could trust). It's not so much the guy who makes the alarm bells ring, but more the *circumstances* he wants to put you in. Remember you don't have to trust a guy to have a dance with him, you don't have to trust a guy to have a chat with him, and you don't have to trust a guy to put your arm around him, but if you're going outside or away from your friends with him, then you have to be able to trust him. It's at this point you have to be able to step back and ask yourself 'What makes me believe I can trust this guy?' I think in most cases this 'trust' is given based on *how* the guy has been acting towards you, which is exactly my point: he may well be just *acting*. In most cases you may not know until it's a little too late.

The bottom line here is to really evaluate what leads you to believe that you can trust somebody enough to leave the safety of your friends, or a populated environment, and go somewhere with them. It's not a case of being paranoid, just cautious. Let's not forget that for young women between the ages of 15 and 25, it is social environments like parties and nightclubs that are statistically the most dangerous.

Always be thinking ahead, and ask yourself 'How can

I be sure that when I go with this guy he will be prepared to stop when I ask him to?'

Just remember that the guys who are the biggest problem are the ones who are the most difficult to identify. They are extremely good at making you believe they can be trusted; they'll tell you exactly what they know you want to hear.

Let's illustrate this with a scenario based on an incident that occurred in one of our capital cities a few years ago.

One Saturday night a group of young women were out together at a well-known nightclub in the city. During the evening they met up with a group of guys who joined them at their table and bought the girls a round of drinks. Over the next few hours one of the young women was getting on well with one of the guys. He asked if she would like to join him for a cup of coffee at a café a short distance away. The young woman, obviously thinking he was a nice guy, was happy to accept the invitation and told her girlfriends that they were heading off for a bite and would be back in about half an hour. She got them to promise that they wouldn't leave without her. It was then 1 a.m. and she said she would be back by 2 a.m. at the latest.

The couple headed out of the nightclub towards the café, a walk of no more than 150 metres in a heavily populated area. As they approached the café the guy suggested that rather than waiting to get a seat they head up to a coffee lounge high within a neighbouring skyscraper which was always quiet and had a great view over the city. The young woman agreed. The pair headed through the foyer of the hotel and into the lift. The young woman didn't know it but there was no such coffee lounge in the building, but of course she had no reason to suspect the guy or think anything was wrong; she wouldn't have left the nightclub with him if she didn't believe she could trust him.

The lift doors open at what should have been the correct floor to reveal a corridor with rooms going off it — no coffee lounge. Obviously at this stage the young woman began to get concerned, but the guy was more than prepared for this reaction and reassured her he had mistaken the floor and that the coffee lounge must be the next floor up. He suggests that rather than wait for the lift, now heading back down to the foyer to return, they take the fire stairs up to the next level. Having come this far, and believing it was a genuine mistake, the young woman agreed.

They walked to the stairwell, the guy opened the door and the young woman walked in. Once inside the stairwell the guy grabbed her by the shoulders, pinned her against the wall and started saying something like 'Come on, let's do it, we'll do it here, no one will see'. It became quite obvious to the young woman that this guy had set this whole situation up to get her away from her friends and have sex with her.

It would have taken them no more than three to four minutes to get from the nightclub to the stairwell of the highrise building. So a few minutes earlier this young woman was in a nightclub with over 300 people, among them her closest girlfriends. She is now in the stairwell of a hotel with a guy who is about to rape her. This highlights how easy it can be to move from a relatively safe environment to a potentially volatile one. What happened next is every woman's nightmare.

In the stairwell the young woman made it very clear to the guy that she wasn't interested in his advances, and wanted to go back to her girlfriends. Unfortunately the more she resisted the more violent he became.

The confrontation ended with him punching her so that she fell down a flight of stairs. He then kicked her to death. After this he caught a taxi home.

Back at the nightclub the young woman's girlfriends had started to get concerned as two o'clock turned to three o'clock, then three-thirty, then four o'clock and she still hadn't come back. They headed out onto the street and checked other nightclubs, bars and cafés in an attempt to find her. A cleaner discovered the young woman's body later that morning.

A short time later the guy was arrested and charged with murder. When asked why he had done what he had, he said 'I'd been buying her drinks all night; she just kept saying "No"; I was getting really pissed off'. He is now serving 12 years in prison.

This tragedy was a result of a young woman meeting up with a young guy in a crowded city nightclub and simply walking up the road with him to have a cup of coffee. I often tell this story during my seminars and add that I can understand if people react by thinking: 'Well, that's a terrible story, and it happened in an environment that my girlfriends and I are familiar with, but I'd never leave a nightclub with a guy like that'. I respect that viewpoint but would ask: a guy like *what*? A guy you meet while out with a group of your friends. A guy who bought you a couple of drinks and had a few dances with you. A guy who made the innocent suggestion that you walk 100 metres up the road in one of the busiest streets in the city to have a coffee with him. You wouldn't have left with him?

I have also had people say to me 'You'd be able to suss out a guy like that. After a couple of hours together you'd be able to pick that sort of guy'. I wish that were the case. If it was that easy to pick these guys perhaps we wouldn't be faced with the disturbing statistic that nine out of ten women in this age group who are raped are raped by guys they thought they could trust.

I'm not about to suggest that if you leave a nightclub with a bloke it will end in this kind of horror, but I will say that this situation started out in exactly the same way as every date rape that has ever been reported to me: a guy makes the woman believe he can be trusted. He innocently suggests that they head off for a coffee, or just a bit of fresh air, or offers her a lift home. The woman accepts, thinking everything is fine. Once they're alone he starts to put pressure on her sexually; she resists; he continues, believing he is entitled to get what he is after due to the 'work' he has put in during the night. And the rest you know.

Let's now put all this information together and look at a strategy to use in a date rape situation. The following strategy, as with all those I teach, may not work in every single situation, but in my opinion is still the best option to take.

The date rape strategy

Imagine finding yourself in the following situation:

You've been at a party with a group of friends when you decide it's time to head home. The guy who brought you to the party agrees and offers you a lift, which you accept. After a short drive you find yourself outside your home where you either live alone or no-one else is home for the night. After a brief chat outside you ask the guy if he would like to come in for a coffee. The invitation is accepted, and you both head inside.

After showing him through to the lounge room you put on a CD before going to the kitchen to make the coffee. Let's assume that at this stage you are obviously quite happy to be alone with this guy. You have been out casually a couple of times and enjoyed his company. On each occasion he has been nothing other than a gentleman and so, understandably, you feel very relaxed about spending some quiet time together.

You now return to the lounge room with the coffee and sit down alongside him on the couch.

Let's say that you're quite prepared to have a bit of a kiss and a cuddle on the couch, but equally you are adamant that, at this stage, things will certainly go no further. So you have a very clear idea of how far you are prepared to go. What you're about to discover is that this guy's expectation of you sexually is far greater than you are comfortable with. However, at this stage everything seems fine.

After some idle chatter he makes his first move: the

classic 'stretching of the arms prior to casually draping one over her shoulder' technique. Sensing an absence of resistance, he presses on. The right arm is brought into action to join forces with its 'casually draped' left counterpart. From this strategic vantagepoint a barely detectable slide along the couch sees his lips firmly planted on yours. What a master of seduction.

At this stage you might have no problem with the situation as his actions are well within your comfort zone. However, he is far from satisfied. After five to ten minutes, what started out as a very amiable exchange starts to become a little one-sided. You become aware that the atmosphere in the room has intensified. There is now a distinct tension and urgency in his body language, including a firmer than necessary grip on your shoulders. The charming, polite guy that you happily invited into your lounge room has evolved into a 90 kg, semi-drunken, sexually overactive arsehole who has you pinned down, World Wrestling Federation style, on your couch.

It's at about this time you will ask yourself *the* question that is asked by every girl or woman who find themselves in a conflict situation: 'What the hell do I do to get out of this?'

Step one — Tell him 'No'

Having discovered that you are sharing a couch with a guy whose sexual expectations may far exceed your own, your first step is to *verbally* convey to him that you want him to stop. The first step in the strategy, therefore, is to say 'NO'. I realise that this may sound a little ironic coming from a person who went to great lengths at the start of the chapter to convince you that saying 'No' would not stop a date rape, but *at this stage* you're not dealing with a date rape. At this stage you are simply dealing with a guy who is *trying* to go a little further than what you are comfortable with, a guy who may well be oblivious to the fact that you want him to stop. My suggestion therefore is to *tell* him.

Let's make the difference here between you *thinking* that you want the guy to stop doing what he is doing, and actually *telling* him to stop what he is doing. He can't read your mind. If you want him to stop you must *tell* him to stop. Don't presume that he will interpret silence on your part as a 'red light'. It may well be interpreted as a 'green light' by a guy who mistakenly thinks 'If she hasn't told me to stop, then obviously she wants me to continue'.

So my advice is to say no, and to say it early. If you're feeling uncomfortable and you want the guy to stop, you must *tell* him. The earlier you communicate with him, the earlier the situation may be sorted out.

Let me say at this stage that I believe *most* guys in this type of situation *will* actually stop when you ask them to, because in *most* of these situations you will be right in your evaluation of the guy being trustworthy. But 'most' guys doesn't mean 'all' guys. There are obviously situations when saying 'No' simply doesn't work — that's when you need a strategy.

The other reason I would suggest saying 'No', is that it is an extremely effective way to identify the *type* of guy you are up against. He either respects you, or he doesn't.

The quickest and most effective way to identify which type you are dealing with is simply to ask him to stop what he is doing. The guy who respects you will start to pull back; the guy who doesn't respect you, when, confronted by 'No, no, no', will start to push forward.

Step two — Gauge his reaction

Having made it very clear to the guy that you want him to stop, the next step is to simply gauge his reaction. Let's presume that the more you ask him to stop the more persistent he becomes.

Now you are dealing with a potential date rape situation. Quite clearly the 'No' strategy has passed its use-by date. The guy now has you firmly pinned down on the couch with no intention of going anywhere until he gets what he wants. At about this stage you realise that not only is saying 'No' not working, but it is actually making the situation worse. So you now take the third step in the strategy.

Step three — Get inside his head

The third step in the strategy is, by now, a relatively familiar one if you have read the preceding chapters. Having established that saying 'No' is not working, but is in fact making the situation worse, you need to question *why* it's not working. It's because of what's going on inside the head of the guy you are dealing with.

So let's get inside the head of the guy and look at the situation from his perspective. Only by doing this can we select an appropriate strategy to use against him.

As the guy hears 'No, no, no', it turns into 'She can't say "No" to me, she can't say "No" to me'. The more you say 'No' to this guy the more he justifies his attempts to make you say 'Yes', and hears the little voice inside his head telling him, 'She can't say "No" to you; what's wrong with her? Come on, mate, you've been out with her a couple of times; you've had a good night tonight; you gave her a lift home; she's the one who invited you back here — of course she wants it. Come on; what about all the boys? You told them tonight was the night. You can't wimp out now. Don't listen to all that "No, no" bullshit, they all say "No"; just get into it; she'll be right. Make her say "Yes"; come on, make her say "Yes"'. And throughout all this all he can hear is 'No, no, no'.

Don't think I'm in any way attempting to condone the way the guy is acting. I'm not; I'm simply highlighting *why* he is acting the way he is. The more you know about how he thinks the more equipped you are to deal with it.

Options

If you now step back and look at this situation you can identify what other options are available:

- **Keep saying 'No'** In my opinion if it hasn't worked up until now, and the situation is getting worse, continuing to say 'No' will only compound the situation. Saying 'No' is not the answer.
- **Submit** I don't know one woman who would *willingly* submit to this situation. Submission will of course lead to the guy doing whatever he wants to do and more than likely committing sexual assault. Sadly, submis-

sion is often seen as the only option if saying 'No' hasn't worked.

- **Physically fight back** Although the old left, left, right combination to the guy's head sounds fine in theory, in practice it appears to be a strategy that few girls and women see as being realistic at *this stage* of the confrontation. That's not to say a full-on physical attack wouldn't work, but rather that most women would consider it a last-resort technique. For that reason I would suggest that, unless you feel otherwise, physically attacking the guy may be moved a little further down the queue. Although this is in stark contrast to the approach I suggested for the stranger rapist, remember we are dealing with a totally different type of offender here and this needs to be factored into your selection of strategy.

So if you don't keep saying 'No', you don't submit, and you don't fight back, what the hell do you do? I would suggest step four.

Step four — Tell him 'Yes'

Tell him 'Yes'? That's right, tell him 'Yes'. Stop saying 'No' and start saying 'Yes'. Go along with it and let him think he's won. Now, before you start ripping up the book and hurling it out the window, just bear with me and I'll explain why I believe saying 'Yes' is the best strategy.

In our situation you have been saying 'No' for the last five to ten minutes and what has happened? The guy has become more and more persistent and aggressive and the situation has worsened. Why? Because the more you say

'No' the more he believes he is justified in making you say 'Yes'. He was a nice guy at the party, a nice guy when he gave you a lift home, a nice guy when you invited him inside, and a nice guy when you started having a kiss and a cuddle on the couch. But what happened to the 'nice guy' when you told him 'No'? The 'nice guy' turned into a creep. Why? Because the 'nice guy' had started to lose control over a situation that he believed he was justified in controlling. It's not so much the word 'no' that's the problem here, but rather how the guy in a date rape situation *reacts* to it.

The more he hears 'No' the more he tells himself he's entitled to make you say 'Yes'. So my suggestion at this stage would be to start saying 'Yes'. Surely if the word 'no' is what's making him aggressive, and in turn making the situation worse, then the opposite must calm him down and make the situation better. Think about it: if 'No, no, no' makes him *think* 'Make her say "Yes", make her say "Yes"', then wouldn't 'Yes, yes, yes', make him think, 'Gee, I'm a smooth bastard, look at that; I knew she really wanted it.'

I know some of you are thinking that this is too easy, and no guy's going to fall for it, but stay with me; we're not done yet. I understand why you may think this way, because you're looking at this situation through the eyes of the woman involved, not the guy.

Let me share a couple of trade secrets with you with regard to how these guys think in this type of situation. When a guy is invited in for coffee after a night out he doesn't think that the moment you walk into the lounge room you will fling yourself onto the couch in the starfish position and say, 'Come on, let's get into it!' He expects things to move along slowly as he gradually tests the waters. At this stage he may actually *expect* some resistance from you, but he also believes that at this point he is entitled to press on. This is the guy who believes that when you say 'No' you really mean 'Yes'. This is the guy who actually believes that after he puts a bit of pressure on you that you will come around, and that he's done nothing wrong. He believes that you will eventually say 'Yes'. So when you say 'Yes' this guy doesn't think he's falling for anything; you're just doing what he believes all women do in this situation.

So tell him what he wants to hear and look at how he starts to calm down and relax. Remember this guy has been playing the game all night called 'Make her think I can be trusted'. Well, now you have to start playing a game. Your game's called 'Let him think he's won'. The more he thinks he has control, the more he starts to relax, and the more he starts to relax the more control *you're* getting.

I will just add a couple of other points at this stage to clear up any lingering doubts that you may have. Firstly, when I suggest that you stop saying 'No' and start saying 'Yes', I'm not suggesting you say 'No, no, no, no, no — yes!' but rather that you *act* in a way that makes him believe that he has won. My whole philosophy of self-protection is based on identifying your opponent's weakness and exploiting it with a strategy. The weaknesses of the date rapist are his ego and his ignorance. His ego is what is pushing him to have sex because it can't handle being rejected, and his ignorance makes him believe that he is entitled to get it. Therefore when I suggest that you say 'Yes' what I'm really saying is that you exploit his ego and his ignorance. Let him think he's won, serve up a bit of what he wants to hear: the 'Mmm, that's nice. But you promise you won't tell your friends. Look, I'm not usually like this, but . . . ' sort of stuff. As I write this I know I'm stepping out on the edge and going against most feminist thinking but this 'acting' is just a *strategy* designed to target the ego and ignorance of a guy who is about to rape you. In a nutshell this guy will nearly always fall for the 'girlie' approach simply because it's exactly what he expected.

The second point I would make at this time is about confusing the strategy of this situation with 'consent'. This point is often raised in my seminars when women, understandably, question the virtue of saying 'Yes' to a date rapist when he could later say in a courtroom environment that you consented and therefore he had done nothing wrong.

Firstly let me reiterate that saying 'Yes' is *not* consent in the eyes of the law unless the permission was given freely without the presence of threats, force, violence or coercion. Therefore, from a legal perspective, what I am suggesting is not consent, but *submission*, since you only said 'Yes' as a result of continuously saying 'No' and finding that this was making the situation worse.

Secondly, the strategy I am suggesting is designed to get you out of a potential rape situation, not to deal with possible cross-examination from a defence lawyer in a courtroom some 12 to 18 months after the event. Don't

lose sight of the fact that in this situation you have literally minutes to make a decision and act. Saying 'No' is
clearly making the situation worse; you don't really have
too many other options.

So do we agree that saying 'Yes' at this time is more
than likely to have the desired effect? Great; let's move
on. When you have said 'Yes' the guy starts to relax,
because he thinks he's won. At this stage you don't *stay*
on the couch and wait for the inevitable to occur; you hop
off the couch and walk out of the lounge room. Hang on,
hang on; I know what you're thinking: 'Right, like he's
just going to let you hop off the couch and walk out of the
lounge room!' Yes he is, but to understand *why* you have
to keep thinking like a bloke. He *is* going to let you get
up off the couch and walk out because you *precede* doing
this by telling him that now you have agreed to having
sex with him you have to visit the one room in the house
that almost every guy I know believes all women have to
go to before and after sex. The bathroom.

*Tell him you have to go somewhere that he is quite
prepared to let you go because he believes it is to his advantage.* Tell him you have to go to the bathroom.

If at this stage he is stupid enough to ask you 'What
are you going to the bathroom for?' — unlikely as that is
— I wouldn't worry too much. You're not dealing with a
Rhodes scholar here; simply say to him 'what do you
mean, "what am I going to the bathroom for", we're going
to have sex aren't we? Gee, you're a bugger; stop it!' and
then just head out of the lounge room. Remember he
won't let you go anywhere while he's got the 'no' head on,

but once he's got the 'yes' head on he's putty in your hands.

Now, just to eliminate any confusion, having got out of the lounge room you don't *actually* go to the bathroom, you just *tell* him you are because it's more effective than telling him you're going to head out the back door and contact the police! Once you're out of the lounge room get out, go, leave, get yourself to safety; anywhere is preferable to being in the same house as a guy who, 30 seconds ago, was about to rape you.

A common objection I get at this stage is 'What, you mean just leave? Get out of the house and just leave the guy there?' Yes. That's exactly what I mean. Why would you want to stay in the same house with the guy? 'But you can't just leave the guy in the house!' Why not? What's he going to do: nick your telly? My point is that anywhere is safer than staying in the house. If you're not in the house he can't get to you; if he can't get to you he can't rape you. Isn't this the desired outcome? I accept that this is a somewhat drastic measure, but far less drastic than the consequences of staying in the house. Having left the lounge room, get out of the house, go to a neighbour or somewhere where there are people. Anywhere is safer than staying in the house. If there is only an exit that the guy can see, or it's deadlocked, just getting away long enough to scream or phone for help is better than submitting.

Almost every woman I have spoken to who has gone through a date rape has said if she'd been able to get away she would have, but the guy just wouldn't let her go. I believe this strategy is extremely effective in creating an opportunity to escape, which is the one thing every woman is focusing on in this type of confrontation.

The other reason I strongly advise using the 'yes' strategy is that even if it doesn't work you've lost nothing. Think about it: if you were to say 'Yes' and the guy calmed down, but you were still not able to get away, you have the same two options available to you had you not even tried the strategy: fight him off physically or submit. By trying the 'yes' strategy you are simply *lessening* your reliance on having to fight your way out or being forced into submission.

Of course not all situations are as straightforward as this example. However, the 'yes' strategy can be very effectively adapted to any date rape environment.

Changing the script

If the environment, or circumstances, are other than those outlined in the previous example a simple change of script may be required. If, for example, you are unable to convince the guy to let *you* go somewhere that he thinks is to his advantage, you may have to look at getting him to go somewhere *with you* that he thinks is to his advantage, but which is actually to yours.

A good example of this would be to look back at a scenario similar to the one we discussed earlier where the young woman found herself trapped in a stairwell with a guy who refused to let her go.

In this case, let's imagine that a man has led a woman out of a nightclub on a similar pretence, has taken her into a blind alley and is standing blocking the only way out. She is repeatedly asking the guy to stop and to let her go and her requests are falling on deaf ears as the guy becomes more persistent and aggressive the more he hears 'No'.

With this in mind let's apply the 'yes' strategy and look at the probable change in outcome. Let's presume that, having realised saying 'No' was not only failing but in fact making the situation worse, the young woman started to adopt the 'yes' strategy.

She starts to allow the guy to think he has won by saying 'Okay, okay, settle down, settle down; I don't mean "No" I don't want to have sex with you; of course I want to have sex with you. I left the nightclub with you, didn't I? I just didn't think you were going to bring me to a dirty, filthy, stinking alleyway. Look, I wasn't saying goodbye to my friends because I'm *really* going back in half an hour, give me some credit; of course I want to have some fun with you, but here in an alley?' At this point I believe the 'yes' strategy has effectively de-escalated the situation to the point where the guy has calmed down and relaxed simply because he thinks he has won. The young woman has very effectively verbalised what the guy was thinking and lulled him into a false sense of security.

But, of course, she's still in the alley and far from being safe, so let's continue with the strategy:

'I thought we were going to have a drink? I was going to try and pluck up enough courage to invite you back to my place. I live in a unit here in town. We could be there in a cab in about two minutes. I was hoping you'd want to come back to my place and stay the night. But look, if you'd rather just do it here and get it over and done with, fine, then I'll head back to the nightclub, but I was really hoping we could jump in a cab and head home.' So the issue is no longer whether or not the young woman wants to have sex with the guy, but rather the location.

Not only do I believe that this approach would have totally de-escalated the situation, but I also believe the guy would have taken the young woman by the hand, walked out of the alley and back into a public street — one with plenty of people around. Not because he has suddenly become a 'good bloke', not because he suddenly respects the young woman and not because he has suddenly realised the error of his ways, but simply because he thinks he has *won*. He believes he is now heading back to her house for the night.

While they are walking out, ever closer to other people and safety, he is busy congratulating himself for the great job he has done and working out what he is going to tell the boys and the young woman is still playing the game, stroking the ego, knowing that in a few seconds time they will be among shops, pedestrians, bouncers on the doors of nightclubs, etc. And then she's safe. Not only has the 'yes' strategy removed her out of a potentially volatile situation, but also it has enabled her to get to safety, all the time allowing the guy to think he has won and has total control over the situation.

Having got herself to a more populated area I would advise making contact with a person or people who are in a position to give some form of assistance, for example another woman or women, door/hotel staff at any available club or bar, or if possible police or security staff.

In summary, the 'yes' strategy can be adapted to most environments where date rape is likely to occur. The basic philosophy remains the same even if the script needs to be adjusted. Remember, once the guy thinks he has won and starts to calm down the next step is to either allow him to let you go somewhere that he thinks is to his advantage, or get him to go somewhere with you.

Summary

- Try saying 'No'. Say it early and let him know you're not happy with what he is doing.
- If saying 'No' works, fine, you don't have a problem. If it doesn't work, at least you have identified the type of guy you are dealing with.
- If saying 'No' is not working, understand it's because you're up against a guy who believes he is entitled to get what he wants and is not about to take 'No' for an answer.
- Having established the mind-set you're dealing with, stop saying 'No' and start saying 'Yes'. Let him think he has won. Exploit his weakness: ego and ignorance.
- Having said 'Yes' and seen him relax, simply continue doing what he *expects* you to do — tell him you have to go to the bathroom. Your focus is one way or the other getting yourself to a safer

location. The key here is to allow him to let you go somewhere that he thinks is to his advantage, which is actually to yours. In the 'house' scenario the bathroom is the obvious choice. In other situations, persuade him to go somewhere with you that is safer.

I accept that the 'Yes' strategy may not work in *every* situation. No strategy does, but in my opinion it will work more effectively than any other strategy I have had suggested to me in all the years I have been teaching it. Remember, even if it fails you've lost nothing by trying it.

I am often asked if I cover the topic of date rape with the guys I lecture to and the answer is yes, I do. There are an increasing number of schools and universities that employ me to lecture on this topic to their male students. I believe totally that date rape is a 'male problem' and that there is a lot of room for increased education to guys on this subject. However, I'm also a realist and I accept that this situation is not going to change overnight and accordingly the sort of strategies I have covered in this chapter must continue to be provided for women.

You don't need to be paranoid, just cautious. Remember that parties, pubs and nightclubs aren't usually dangerous in themselves, but the decisions that you make about who you leave with and what circumstances you put yourself into can be. Don't be afraid to stop and question the choices you make and never ignore your intuition.

7

DEFENSIVE STRIKES

Having examined every type of male to female conflict in the previous chapters it is now time to look into some simple, effective and proven physical self defence techniques.

However, before we launch into the techniques of punching, kicking, yelling, screaming and generally going berserk, I will take a few quiet moments to raise a couple of points with regard to physical self defence.

I have long believed that one of the greatest barriers for women with regard to self-protection is the constant suggestion that in order to protect themselves they must have the ability to overpower their attacker physically. This suggestion is not only totally incorrect but extremely damaging because it creates the belief that in a male to female conflict the only option apart from submission is to physically *overpower* an attacker who is almost invariably physically stronger. Of course women do not have to physically overpower a male attacker in order to get to safety but rather to follow the basic principle behind effective self defence, the principle to which this book is devoted:

Don't focus on your opponent's strength and submit to it — identify his weakness and exploit it with a strategy.

Up until now we have applied this principle to understanding the *psychology* behind the confrontation and the mind-set of the offender. In this chapter we will apply it in a physical sense.

The *physical* aspect of self-protection is not the hard part. The hard part is having the ability to stay calm, focus on an outcome and select the right strategy. In reality, with those three elements in place, the physical act of smashing somebody is actually quite easy! I think far too much time and energy is spent on teaching people how to deliver a 'textbook' punch, or perfect strike to the groin when, in fact, with sufficient motivation and self-belief the majority of women I know have more than enough ability to physically defend themselves.

Effective physical self defence should not rely on overpowering your attacker, but rather targeting his vulnerable areas in such a way that his attention turns away from you and back on to himself, enabling you to get away.

The following defensive strikes have been selected with this in mind.

Remember, in a potentially volatile situation with unknown, unarmed offender(s), if you can run, you should get to somewhere safe and make as much noise as possible along the way. (Strategies against both the armed offender and the acquaintance rapist are outlined in previous chapters.) But if you can't run, all the research indicates that the next best options are to verbally and physically confront the offender. If ever you find yourself in this type of confrontation, and you make the decision to fight back, here are some strikes that you may find useful.

Basic defensive strikes

Yelling

▨ One of the most effective defences against the unarmed stranger offender is to simply make as much noise as you can. Remember, the greatest fear this type of offender has is getting caught, so yell and scream as much as you can.

All the following strikes should be combined with you yelling at the offender. I find that in my courses shouting the word 'NO!' is a very effective way to generate noise and aggression as each strike is delivered.

Eye strike (figure 1)

▨ Without doubt the eyes are the most vulnerable area of any attacker. Once the eyes have been attacked there is little if any chance of him preventing you getting away.

▨ The most effective way of attacking the eyes is to form the hand into a claw and grab hold of the offender's face.

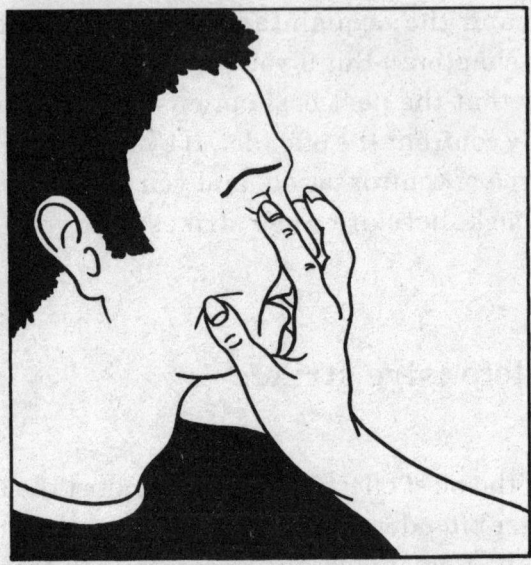

Figure 1: Eye strike

- Once you have hold of the face, gouge at the eyes with any available fingers. This type of attack is extremely painful and will cause temporary blindness, enabling you to escape.

Nose strike (figure 2)

- The nose is an excellent target as it breaks easily, is extremely painful when hit, and when struck severely impairs the offender's vision.
- The most effective way to strike an offender's nose is with a 'heel-palm' strike. This is achieved by holding your hand with the fingers curled back into a 'cat's claw' and making contact with the heel of the palm.

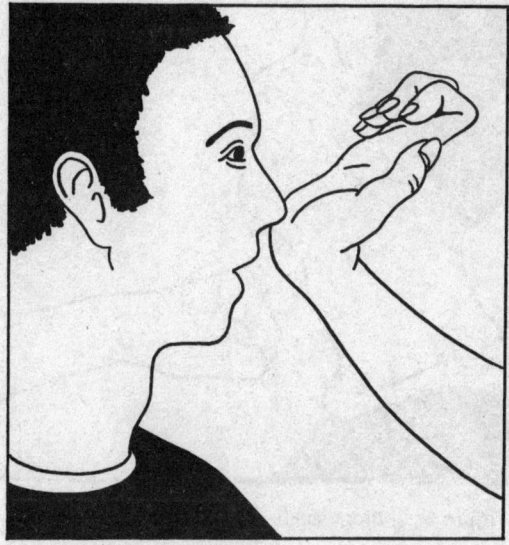

Figure 2: Nose strike

- The strike comes from the shoulder and is very effective against a taller opponent.

Throat strike (figure 3)

- If you have ever received a punch or elbow in the throat you will know why I include this in my defensive strikes. A well-directed strike to this area can smash the larynx and cause excruciating pain.
- A correct fist must be made (thumb folded over index finger), and your wrist must be straight and firm.
- Don't punch *at* the target, but rather *through* it to maximise the effect of the strike.

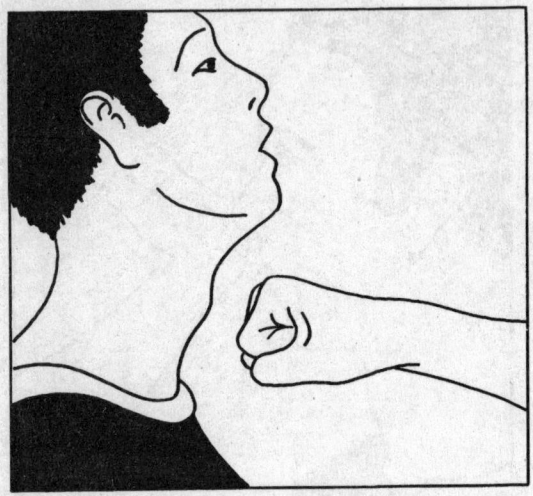

Figure 3: Throat strike

Groin strike (figure 4)

■ Ah yes, the old favourite. Of all the strikes I teach in my courses this one requires the least tuition! There is no doubt that a well-executed strike to the groin of a male offender will bring him crashing to his knees and the thought of any further activity involving this part of his anatomy will be far from his mind. However, as with all things, there is a right and a wrong way to go about it.

■ Firstly, the groin is seldom a 'primary' target at the initial point of contact, meaning there are usually other vulnerable areas more easily attacked (i.e. eyes, nose or throat). But the groin is an extremely vulnerable area if it presents itself for attack.

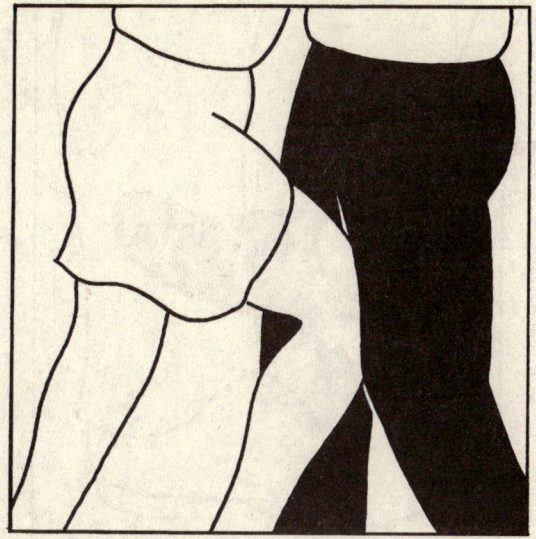

Figure 4: Groin strike

▧ Secondly, forget the old wives' tale about 'kneeing 'em where it hurts'. Your knee, or more specifically your patella, is not a particularly large area and neither is the area you are targeting. My suggestion would be that if you're close enough to go for the groin, grab hold of his shirt, pull yourself up and in towards him and make contact with your *thigh*, not your knee.

▧ You should focus on projecting your weight *up* and slightly *forward*. Imagine him wearing his testicles as earrings, direct your thigh upwards towards them and you won't be too far from the mark.

Foot strike (figure 5)

▧ The feet are seldom seen as likely targets when listing vulnerable areas yet, surprisingly, they are a very

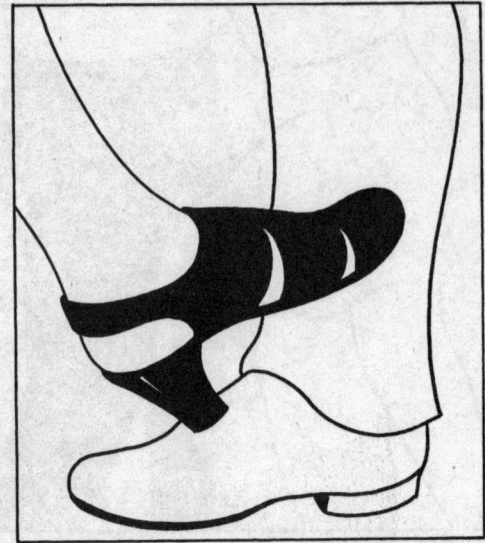

Figure 5: Foot strike

effective area to attack — as anyone who has dropped anything heavy onto their foot will attest.

- The key here is to target the *bridge* of the foot rather than the toes. Your target is the metatarsal bones that are between the toes and the ankle.
- The strike is executed by slamming the point of your heel down through the top of the offender's foot. The force generated by such a strike can easily smash the metatarsal bones in the foot.
- Remember that if he is close enough to grab you his feet aren't too far away.

These five strikes can be practised individually or put together as a combination. Remember, as you do each strike to yell 'No' to help make each move nice and aggres-

Figure 6:   Elbow strike — under chin

sive. The whole focus behind these or in fact any defensive strikes is to create an opportunity to escape. Once you have achieved this, continue to make as much noise as you can while getting yourself to safety.

Additional strikes

Although the five strikes outlined above provide more than enough options in an attack situation here are a couple of others you may like to have a go at.

Elbow strike — under chin (figure 6)
■ The elbow strike is a favourite of mine when you really need to do some damage quickly and effectively.

185

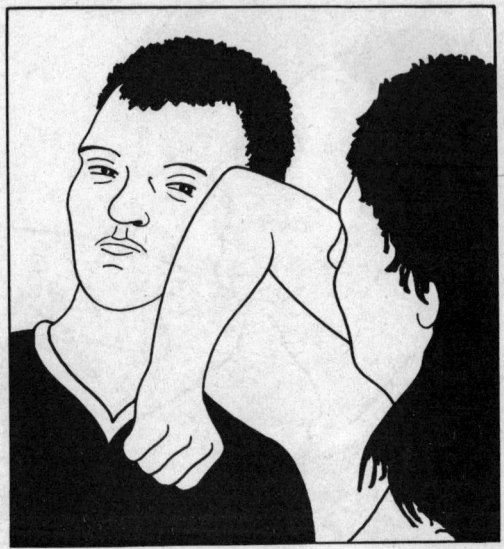

Figure 7: Elbow strike — to side of head or temple

- One advantage of this strike is it generates more power than a conventional punch due to the point of impact being closer to your body.
- The other obvious advantage is that a shorter person can easily execute this strike on a taller opponent.
- The focus should be to make contact directly under the chin with your elbow or forearm. Don't just 'swing' the elbow up to the chin, but really launch into it, using your legs to project real power into the strike.

Elbow strike — to side of head or temple (figure 7)
- As with the elbow strike to the chin, this is an extremely powerful strike when executed correctly.

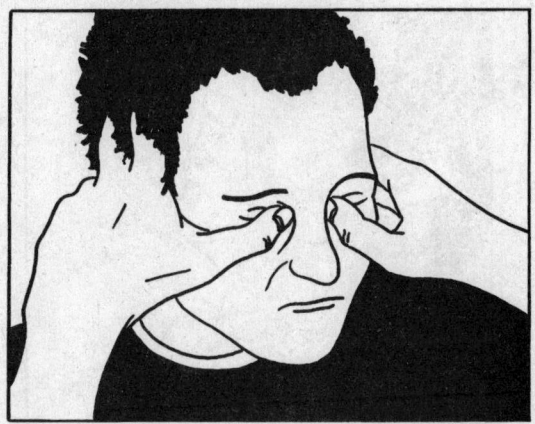

Figure 8: Thumb gouge to eyes

- The focus here is to strike the side of the offender's head around the area of the temple.
- The point of contact is not so much the elbow but rather the forearm. To generate power into the strike don't just 'swing' your arm out but actually rotate your upper body into the strike as you would with a conventional punch.

Thumb gouge to eyes (figure 8)

- Don't practice this one on people you like! The thumb gouge is a very effective way to attack the eyes of an offender.
- As previously mentioned, the eyes are one of the most vulnerable areas in an attack situation.
- This particular method is excellent to use if you have been pinned in any way by the offender.
- Literally grab hold of the offender's face as illustrated

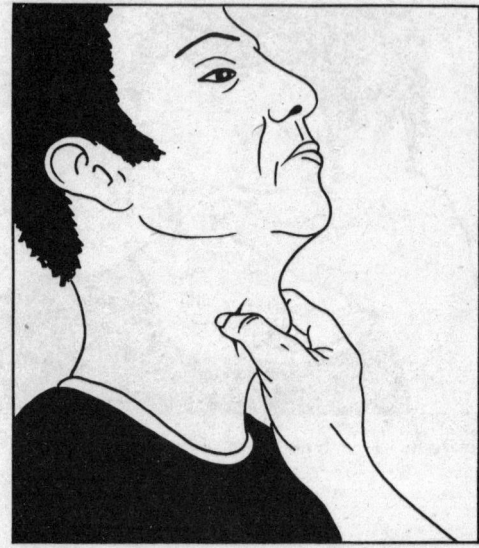

Figure 9: Choker hold to windpipe

and push the thumbs into the eyes either side of the nose. Push the thumbs 'in' and 'out' to maximise the effect.

Choker hold to windpipe (figure 9)

■ This is an effective variation on the infamous police choker hold used to render violent offenders unconscious. Unlike the police version, which is applied from behind using the arm, this hold is simply applied by squeezing the offender's windpipe with your hand. Although unlikely to render him unconscious, this hold is painful and effective when correctly applied.

■ Focus on the area of the adam's apple. Drive the fingers

in behind the windpipe and squeeze for all you're worth.

■ Along with the thumb gouge to the eyes, this is a handy one to use if pinned or held close to the offender.

Defending against the attack from behind

Being attacked from behind reduces the range of options available to you but certainly does not mean you cannot defend yourself. Bear in mind that the offender who grabs you from behind is even more gutless than the idiot who confronts you face-to-face. Any form of defence used against this guy is totally unexpected and has maximum impact.

Groin attack from behind (figure 10)

■ This is simply a full on attack to the offender's groin.

■ It goes without saying that any attack of this nature is both excruciatingly painful and extremely effective. As opposed to the frontal attack where the groin is not as exposed, any attack from behind leaves this area totally vulnerable.

■ The focus here is to get your arm in behind you and grab a nice big handful of testicles. This is best achieved by reaching 'up' into the groin from beneath the scrotum.

■ Once the hand is in place, squeeze the testicles, twist the scrotum, and pull as if you are 'ripping' the groin out and down. Earplugs are optional to soften the impact of the bloodcurdling screams.

■ Just one last point — don't let go until he does. But don't worry, you won't have to wait long.

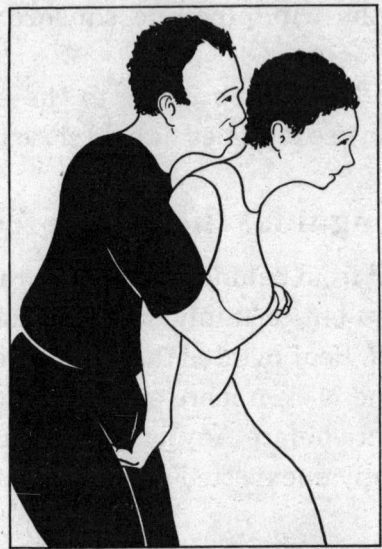

Figure 10 Groin attack from behind

Reverse head butt (figure 11)

▓ This head butt is a variation on what is affectionately known as the 'Liverpool Kiss'. The principle here is if he's close enough to grab you, you're close enough to slam the back of your head into his face.

▓ Unlike the closely related 'frontal head butt' the reverse version doesn't pose the risk of miscalculating and breaking your own nose!

▓ The trick here is to accurately gauge where the offender's head is positioned as you'll probably only get one or two cracks at it before he cottons on to what you're doing and moves out of range.

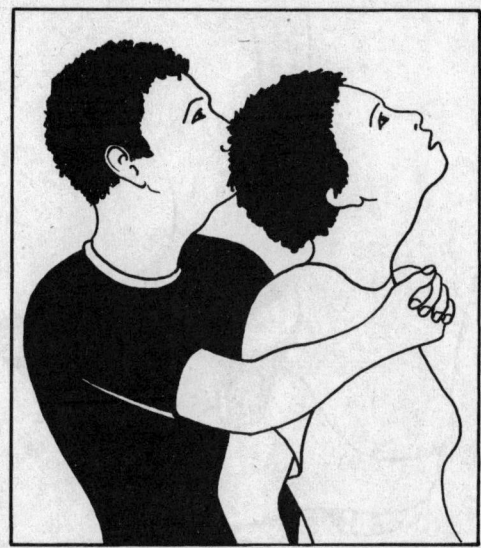

Figure 11: Reverse head butt

■ The execution is pretty simple — just throw your head back into his face as forcefully as you can. This sort of contact can easily break a nose, crack a cheek bone, split an eyebrow, cut lips and break teeth.

■ It would be extremely unlikely to knock yourself out executing this strike as the back of your head can withstand a great deal more force than the offender's face can. While policing I have copped a couple of these myself from male offenders, and can attest to the fact that the butt*ee* comes off a lot worse than the butt*er*.

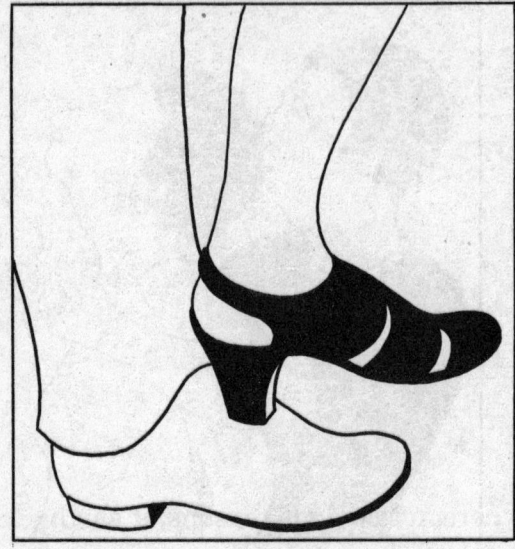

Figure 12: Heel strike to foot behind

Heel strike to foot behind (figure 12)

- This is only a slight variation on the strike to the foot covered earlier. As mentioned, in most attack situations the offender's feet are vulnerable to attack.
- The fundamental difference here is the position of the attacker. However, this does not lessen the effectiveness of the strike.
- Simply slam the heel down onto the offender's foot from the position you're standing in. Remember to target the bridge of the foot to maximise the impact of the strike.

Improvised weapons

If all else fails, just grab anything you can get your hands on and use it as a weapon. The list of everyday items that can be used to attack an offender are limited only by your imagination. Here are a couple that come to mind.

Aerosol sprays

- Basically anything that sprays can be used as a weapon: hairspray, deodorant, or any household spray you can get hold of at short notice such as fly spray or cleaning fluid.
- Simply spray the contents into the offender's eyes. The only drawback is using this method outside on a windy day where, for obvious reasons, it can backfire.

Keys

- Keys have long been the weapon of choice for that scary walk through the dimly lit carpark late at night and with good reason; a quick slash across the face with a handful of keys can really slow an attacker down.
- To get full effect from the keys you position them between the fingers pointing outwards. When you form a fist the keys protrude from between the fingers to make contact with the offender's face.
- When you punch or lash out at the offender the keys scratch and puncture the skin.

Any appliance with a cord

- This is an effective way to keep an offender at bay as well as being used as an actual weapon. Imagine an iron, toaster, bedside clock, or radio being swung around lasso-style in the general direction of the offender's head.

- The technique is to hold the appliance by the cord and swing it in a 'figure eight' formation in front of you. The iron would be my choice of appliance for this method due to its obvious weight and potential to injure.
- If the offender is foolish enough to move into the arc of the appliance at the very least he will become entangled in the swinging cord and with any luck get a good solid whack in the head with whatever happens to be swinging from the end of it.

Dirt/sand/soil

- A handful of dirt, sand or potting mix rubbed into the eyes of an offender may well be just as effective as an eye gouge.
- Obviously, as with all such improvised weapons, the dirt, sand, etc. has to be within arm's reach when you need it, but don't rule it out as a possibility both outside or even inside the house if you have a few pot plants around the place.
- This technique is not only effective when the soil or sand is rubbed into the eyes, but also when it is thrown into the offender's face.

So, as you can see, pretty much anything you can get your hands on can be used as a weapon if need be. I'm not suggesting such improvised weapons replace any of the defensive strikes I have outlined, but rather that they provide a back-up if all else fails.

In summary, let me reiterate that the physical strikes and techniques I have outlined are actually very easy to execute. The real key to effective self defence is having the presence of mind, attitude and motivation to be able to fully exploit the weakness of the offender. I firmly believe that once this mind-set is in place the physical act of defending yourself is simply a natural progression.

One final point with regard to these defensive strikes is to bear in mind that simply *reading* through them will not enable you to execute them effectively. I would strongly suggest that if you feel any or all of these strikes may be of assistance to you in an attack situation that you put some time aside to actually practise using them. This 'practice' needs only to be five to ten minutes once or twice a day for a week or two just to familiarise yourself with the strikes you feel most comfortable with. I promise you that a little bit of effort put in regularly over a relatively short period of time can make all the difference between physically freezing and being able to effectively defend yourself in an attack situation. And never forget, physical self defence is easy, but only if you *believe* you can do it.

8

QUESTIONS AND
ANSWERS

In this book I have tried to answer the basic fundamental question of self defence, the question every person asks in every conflict situation. The question is 'What do I have to do to get out of this?' Your ability to answer this question is what ultimately determines your ability to defend yourself.

Self defence is simply your ability to answer this key question. And this will be determined by the knowledge that you take into the situation. I hope the knowledge you have gained from this book will increase your ability to deal with the situations I have outlined.

The information in those previous chapters might have sparked a few related questions, so to conclude here are the most frequently asked questions from my seminars, and my answers.

FAQs

1. **Q.** If I did find myself in a confrontational situation and I used some form of physical self defence is there any chance of the offender charging me with assault?

   A. No. The law with regard to self defence is very clear in this type of situation: if you feel genuine fear for your safety, or for the safety of others, you are entitled to use whatever force is reasonable and necessary under the circumstances. Therefore if you find yourself in a situation where you fear for your own personal safety, such as a physical confrontation, you are quite entitled under the law to use any form of reasonable and necessary self defence. In all the time I have worked in this area I have never heard of a woman being charged as a result of defending herself in a genuine confrontational situation.

2. **Q.** You have spoken about the situation of being followed by an offender. How can you tell that you are actually being followed or if it's just a figment of your imagination?

   A. Firstly, if your instinct, or 'gut feeling', is telling you something is wrong then something probably is. Never ignore this basic human instinct. Get in touch with it and increase your awareness of your environment. Secondly, if you need further confirmation that the person 15 to 20 metres behind you is in fact following you I would suggest one of two techniques. Either stop, turn around and make eye contact with him (his body language and general reaction will leave you in no doubt of his intentions), or simply cross the road and continue along the other side of the street, all the time being aware of the guy's movements. Both these simple techniques will very quickly and effectively let you know if further action needs to be taken. If it does, get to somewhere safe.

3. Q. Is it true that it is better to yell 'Fire' than 'Rape' or 'Help' if you are attacked, because people are more likely to take notice if they think there is a fire?

A. I don't really subscribe to this theory for a couple of reasons. Firstly, when I advise people to yell and scream, as I often do, the reason I suggest this is not so much how other people in the vicinity will react but more how the *offender* will react. Secondly, if somebody does come to your aid then that's a bonus but I don't believe that those who ignore the cries of 'Rape' or 'Help' will suddenly come running because they hear 'Fire'. I don't really think it matters what you yell, just so long as you yell.

4. Q. How do you suggest dealing with a flasher?

A. I'd love to say just start laughing, point at his dick and say 'Hey, look, just like a penis, only smaller'. But I'd better not. The flasher is pretty much right down there at the bottom of the food chain, but being confronted by a flasher can still be a frightening or at best disturbing situation. As per the strategies I suggest for unarmed confrontations, I would advise moving to a populated area if possible and verbally drawing attention to the guy's behaviour. If this is not possible and the confrontation occurs in an isolated environment I would advise a firm, assertive, verbal response, for example: 'Piss off and leave me alone you grubby little man, I'm about to call the police to have you taken away'. It is unlikely for this type of offender to progress past this point of the confrontation as most are simply attempting to get a 'shocked' response from their target before running off. Although it's unlikely he will do much more than expose himself — which means you should be able to walk away from him unhindered — this type of behaviour can lead to more serious sexual acts, therefore I would always suggest that this type of behaviour be reported to the police.

5. Q. If I'm on a bus or a train and some guy stands or sits alongside me and starts to touch me or rub up against me should I just ignore it?

  A. No, not unless you want it to continue. If his behaviour is making you feel uncomfortable and his actions are obviously intentional I suggest you move to a more suitable location if one is available. If not, try making a bit of a scene by informing all those within earshot as to what this guy is doing. This is very effective because the guy believed you would be passive and submissive. How can you make sure that his actions *are* intentional? If the contact is accidental I doubt whether it would go beyond one actual physical contact from the guy in question. However, if the physical contact is ongoing I doubt very much that this is anything other than intentional. The bottom line here is not so much the actions/intention on the part of the guy, but rather how you interpret his behaviour. If the behaviour/contact is initially low key then obviously your response would be gauged accordingly, but if it continues your response would perhaps need to become more assertive. If you are being made to feel uncomfortable be prepared to let your feelings be known verbally. Just a quick word about prevention: the safest place to sit on a bus is as close to the driver as you can. On a train the safest carriage is the front one which is occupied by the driver who has radio contact with the transit police, or if there is one, in the carriage indicated as safe in the evening by a blue light or line on the platform.

6. Q. What is the best thing to do if you receive obscene phone calls?

A. Hang up. The idiot on the other end is after a reaction, so don't give him one and he'll usually get bored and move on. If the calls continue or become more sinister in nature contact your phone company and ask their advice. If you don't get any joy there contact the police. Misuse of a telephone is a criminal offence.

7. Q. With so many alarm systems on the market with such varying price tags it's difficult to know what system to pick. Do you have any advice?

A. Let me first say I am certainly no alarm expert and have no affiliation with any company or specific product. My answer is purely based on my own experience and what I would consider for my own family. What is most precious in your home is you and your family so I have always struggled with the idea of spending large amounts of money on an alarm system that only works when you're not in the house! If you have the financial capacity to install an electronic system my advice would be to install one that you can activate while you're *in* the house. This is called a perimeter alarm. While expensive, this system is designed to be activated if somebody attempts to get into your house when you're there. Another handy accessory is a 'panic button' that you can have installed in a useful place, (e.g. your bedroom), which sets off all the bells and whistles when you give it a whack. But moving away from the top end of the market, you can't go past the lights that you can attach to the outside of the house which are activated by movement or heat. I believe they are a very effective deterrent against the offender who wants to gain access to the house undetected, as well as being very cost-effective.

In my experience the most faithful, dependable and fail-safe alarm system of all is the good old family dog barking its head off. It doesn't really seem to matter what type of dog, although I'd rather put the safety of myself and my loved ones in the hands of a 55-kilogram Rottweiler than a Pekinese/terrier cross.

8. Q. Where would you recommend a person goes following a sexual or indecent assault if they require professional advice and/or medical attention?

A. My advice would be to contact either a local rape crisis centre (the number will be listed in the front of the White Pages phone book), or to visit a sexual assault unit. Sexual assault units are located in most major hospitals, are available 24 hours a day and staffed by doctors and counsellors specially trained in this area. Visiting one of these units does not mean that you have to report the incident to the police. However, if you do make that decision the expertise of those who care for you can be called upon in court and their inclusion may well strengthen your case. For information on services in New Zealand call Rape Crisis, Sexual Abuse Help or Counselling Services. They will go with you to the police and to a doctor trained in working with rape survivors (Doctors for Sexual Abuse Care).

9. Q. My boyfriend/husband can easily pin me down or against a wall when we are play wrestling. I can't overpower him, so how could I get away from an attacker?

   A. Remember, 'self defence' does not mean overpowering your attacker, but rather focusing on his weakness and exploiting it with a strategy. Don't confuse what you are prepared to do when fooling around with your boyfriend/husband with what you would be prepared to do in a real attack situation. The obvious advantage your boyfriend/husband has is that he is physically stronger than you are and is safe in the knowledge that you are unlikely to lash out at his vulnerable areas (eyes, nose, throat and groin), therefore he has the upper hand in this situation. Of course in an actual attack situation you should be prepared to do all sorts of nasty, mean things to an offender in order to change the balance of power.

10. Q. Now that I know all this, I'm feeling a lot more confident about my ability to defend myself. Is there any danger of me becoming *overconfident* and lulling myself into a false sense of security?

    A. In my experience women don't seem to suffer from the same false overconfidence and bravado that guys do after throwing one punch at some local karate class and then mistakenly thinking they can now take on the world. I agree there is a thin line between confidence and false bravado, but it is a line seldom crossed by the women I have put through my courses. I never advise anyone to look for, or create a confrontation if it can possibly be avoided. However, if a confrontation is unavoidable I see no problem with you having the confidence and ability to deal with it.

11. Q. Prior to having this information I never really thought much about being attacked or the type of men who commit these crimes. Don't you think all this information can actually *increase* women's fear and make them more paranoid?

A. No, definitely not. If I thought that I certainly wouldn't have devoted the past ten years of my life sharing this information with as many women as possible. As I have mentioned throughout the book, 'fear' is often a state of mind, which is a direct result of conditioning and what you *choose* to believe. If you *choose* to believe that increased knowledge, better understanding and having greater options increases fear then I guess you would be right. However, I much prefer to believe that this information actually increases your level of *awareness*, not your level of fear. Knowledge is certainly nothing to be afraid of, even if some of that knowledge challenges conventional beliefs and takes you out of your comfort zone. It can only make you afraid if you allow it to.

12.Q. Having all this information is great but if I find myself in a conflict situation and I just freeze, then what?

A. I firmly believe the 'freeze' is caused by our inability to answer that fundamental question that defines self-defence, 'What do I have to do to get out of this?' If you find yourself in any type of conflict situation and you are unable to answer this question the most likely result is that you will 'freeze'. The reason behind passing on all the information that is contained in this book is to give you sufficient knowledge to answer this question under the pressure of a confrontational situation. If you have this knowledge, you will avoid freezing. Ultimately we only 'freeze' in situations that we fear, and we are fearful in a situation because we don't know how to deal with it. Knowledge is power and the more of it you take into a situation the less the likelihood of you freezing and losing control.

AFTERWORD

I sincerely hope that you never have to use any of the knowledge and strategies I have outlined. However, if you are confronted by any such situations be reassured that you now do know what to do. I would encourage you to re-visit this book from time to time as retention of knowledge is the key to being able to apply that knowledge. The greater your understanding of how dangerous men think, the greater your ability to stay safe for life.

For more information on women's self-protection and the seminars I conduct please visit my website: www.winningedgestrategies.com.au, email: info@winningedgestrategies.com.au or write to: Brent Sanders, Winning Edge Strategies, care of:

Random House Australia
20 Alfred Street
Milsons Point NSW 2061

or Random House New
 Zealand
18 Poland Road
Glenfield, Auckland

SELECTED BIBLIOGRAPHY

Allison, Julie A. and Wrightson, Lawrence S., *Rape: The Misunderstood Crime*. California: Sage Publications Inc, 1993.

Bart, Pauline B. and O'Brien, Patricia H., *Stopping Rape: Successful Survival Strategies*. New York: Teachers College Press, 1993.

Corbett, Jan, *Caught by his Past*. New Zealand: Tandem Press, 1996.

de Paul, Lynsey and McCormack, Clare, *Taking Control*. Great Britain: Boxtree, 1993.

Frank, Gerold, *The Boston Strangler*. New York: The New American Library Inc, 1966.

Neff, James, *The Pursuit and Capture of a Serial Rapist*. London: Virgin Publishing Ltd, 1995.

Nelson, Joan M., *Self-defense: Steps to Success*, Human Kinetics Publishers, Champaign, Illinois, 1991.

Ressler, Robert K. Burgess, Ann W. and Douglas, John

E., *Sexual Homicide: Patterns and Motives*. Great Britain: Simon & Schuster Ltd, 1993.

Rule, Anne, *The Stranger Beside Me*. Great Britain: Warner Books, 1994.

Smith, Bronilyn, *Self-protection for Women: A Seminar / Workshop Guide for Presenters*, National Agenda for Women Project, 1988.

Weiser Easteal, Patricia (ed), *Without Consent: Confronting Adult Sexual Violence*. Conference proceedings, Australian Institute of Criminology, 1993.

Yallop, David, *Deliver Us from Evil.*' Great Britain: Corgi Books, 1993.

ACKNOWLEDGMENTS

I would like to express my sincere thanks and gratitude to all those people who offered me their support, knowledge and wisdom which has contributed to the creation of this book.

To Tim Curnow at Curtis Brown Literary Agents who convinced me that a book of this nature needed to be written and guided me through those daunting early stages. To all the team at Random House who have supported me 100 per cent from day one, in particular Hazel Flynn and Katie Stackhouse for their encouragement and guidance.

Thanks also to Wayne Hutchins for his illustrations of the various defensive strikes in Chapter Seven.

And finally I must thank the thousands of women and girls who not only attended my seminars over the past ten years, but who provided me with ongoing knowledge and insight into the area of male to female conflict.

Permission acknowledgments

I wish to thank the following authors and publishers for allowing me to use extracts from their publications: David Yallop: *Deliver Us from Evil*, Corgi Books, p.28; Bronilyn Smith: *Self-protection for Women: A Seminar/Workshop Guide for Presenters*, A National Agenda for Women Project, p.44; Sage Publications, Inc: *Rape: The Misunderstood Crime*, Julie A. Allison and Lawrence S. Wrightson, pp.249, 250, 251, 71, 76, 77, 78, 82; Virgin Publishing Ltd, London: *The Pursuit and Capture of A Serial Rapist*, James Neff, p.244; Human Kinetics, Illinois: *Self-defense: Steps to Success*, Joan M. Nelson, pp.15, 31; Warner Books UK: *The Stranger Beside Me*, Ann Rule, p.117; The Teachers College Press, New York: *Stopping Rape: Successful Survival Strategies*, Pauline B. Bart and Patricia H. O'Brien, pp.1, 40, 41, 43, 34, 36, 105, 54; Pan Macmillan UK: *Taking Control: Basic Mental & Physical Self Defence for Women*, Lynsey de Paul and Clare McCormack; Simon & Schuster UK: *Sexual Homicide: Patterns and Motives*, Robert K. Ressler, Ann W. Burgess and John E. Douglas, pp.210-211; William Morris Agency, New York: *The Boston Strangler*, Gerold Frank, p.297; Australian Institute of Criminology: 'Without Consent: Confronting Adult Sexual Violence' (conference proceedings), Patricia Weiser Easteal (ed.).